D1447160

Arthur Schopenhauer

ON HUMAN NATURE

Essays in Ethics and Politics

TRANSLATED BY
Thomas Bailey Saunders

DOVER PUBLICATIONS, INC.
Mineola, New York

Bibliographical Note

This Dover edition, first published in 2010, is an unabridged republication of the Thomas Bailey Saunders translation of the work, originally published by Swan Sonnenschein & Company, London, in 1897 under the title and subtitle *On Human Nature: Essays (Partly Posthumous) in Ethics and Politics.*

Library of Congress Cataloging-in-Publication Data

Schopenhauer, Arthur, 1788-1860.
  On human nature : essays in ethics and politics / Arthur Schopenhauer; translated by Thomas Bailey Saunders.
         p. cm. — (Dover philosophical classics)
  "Unabridged republication of the Thomas Bailey Saunders translation of the work, originally published by Swan Sonnenschein & Company, London, in 1897 under the title and subtitle On Human Nature: essays (partly posthumous) in ethics and politics"—T.p. verso.
English translation from a German original.
  ISBN-13: 978-0-486-47841-8
  ISBN-10: 0-486-47841-6
     1. Ethics.   2. Political science.   I. Saunders, T. Bailey (Thomas Bailey), 1860–1928.   II. Title.
B3118.E5S4 2010
170—dc22

                                                                    2010021595

Manufactured in the United States by LSC Communications
                    47841603   2018
                 www.doverpublications.com

Translator's Preface

This following essays are drawn from the chapters entitled *Zur Ethik* and *Zur Rechtslehre und Politik* which are to be found both in Schopenhauer's *Parerga* and in his posthumous writings. As in my previous volumes, so also in this, I have omitted a few passages which appeared to me to be either antiquated or no longer of any general interest. For convenience' sake I have divided the original chapters into sections, which I have had to name; and I have also had to invent a title which should express their real scope. The reader will find that it is not so much *Ethics* and *Politics* that are here treated, as human nature itself in various aspects.

T.B.S.

November, 1896

Contents

Human Nature

Truths of the physical order may possess much external significance, but internal significance they have none. The latter is the privilege of intellectual and moral truths, which are concerned with the objectivation of the will in its highest stages, whereas physical truths are concerned with it in its lowest.

For example, if we could establish the truth of what up till now is only a conjecture, namely, that it is the action of the sun which produces thermo-electricity at the equator; that this produces terrestrial magnetism; and that this magnetism, again, is the cause of the *aurora borealis,* these would be truths externally of great, but internally of little, significance. On the other hand, examples of internal significance are furnished by all great and true philosophical systems; by the catastrophe of every good tragedy; nay, even by the observation of human conduct in the extreme manifestations of its morality and immorality, of its good and its evil character. For all these are expressions of that reality which takes outward shape as the world, and which, in the highest stages of its objectivation, proclaims its innermost nature.

To say that the world has only a physical and not a moral significance is the greatest and most pernicious of all errors, the fundamental blunder, the real perversity of mind and temper; and, at bottom, it is doubtless the tendency which faith personifies as Anti-Christ. Nevertheless, in spite of all religions—and they are systems which one and all maintain the opposite, and seek to establish it in their mythical way—this fundamental error never becomes quite extinct, but raises its head from time to time afresh, until universal indignation compels it to hide itself once more.

Yet, however certain we may feel of the moral significance of life and the world, to explain and illustrate it, and to resolve the

1

contradiction between this significance and the world as it is, form a task of great difficulty; so great, indeed, as to make it possible that it has remained for me to exhibit the true and only genuine and sound basis of morality everywhere and at all times effective, together with the results to which it leads. The actual facts of morality are too much on my side for me to fear that my theory can ever be replaced or upset by any other.

However, so long as even my ethical system continues to be ignored by the professorial world, it is Kant's moral principle that prevails in the universities. Among its various forms the one which is most in favour at present is "the dignity of man." I have already exposed the absurdity of this doctrine in my treatise on the *Foundation of Morality*.[1] Therefore I will only say here that if the question were asked on what the alleged dignity of man rests, it would not be long before the answer was made that it rests upon his morality. In other words, his morality rests upon his dignity, and his dignity rests upon his morality.

But apart from this circular argument it seems to me that the idea of dignity can be applied only in an ironical sense to a being whose will is so sinful, whose intellect is so limited, whose body is so weak and perishable as man's. How shall a man be proud, when his conception is a crime, his birth a penalty, his life a labour, and death a necessity!—

> *Quid superbit homo? cujus conceptio culpa,*
> *Nasci pœna, labor vita, necesse mori!*★

Therefore, in opposition to the above-mentioned form of the Kantian principle, I should be inclined to lay down the following rule: When you come into contact with a man, no matter whom, do not attempt an objective appreciation of him according to his worth and dignity. Do not consider his bad will, or his narrow understanding and perverse ideas; as the former may easily lead you to hate and the latter to despise him; but fix your attention

---

[1] § 8.

★*Editor's Note:* The English text immediately preceding each of the foreign language quotations contains a full, accurate translation of it, either literal or slightly paraphrased.

only upon his sufferings, his needs, his anxieties, his pains. Then you will always feel your kinship with him; you will sympathise with him; and instead of hatred or contempt you will experience the commiseration that alone is the peace to which the Gospel calls us. The way to keep down hatred and contempt is certainly not to look for a man's alleged "dignity," but, on the contrary, to regard him as an object of pity.

The Buddhists, as the result of the more profound views which they entertain on ethical and metaphysical subjects, start from the cardinal vices and not the cardinal virtues; since the virtues make their appearance only as the contraries or negations of the vices. According to Schmidt's *History of the Eastern Mongolians* the cardinal vices in the Buddhist scheme are four: Lust, Indolence, Anger, and Avarice. But probably instead of Indolence, we should read Pride; for so it stands in the *Lettres édifiantes et curieuses,*[1] where Envy, or Hatred, is added as a fifth. I am confirmed in correcting the statement of the excellent Schmidt by the fact that my rendering agrees with the doctrine of the Sufis, who are certainly under the influence of the Brahmins and Buddhists. The Sufis also maintain that there are four cardinal vices, and they arrange them in very striking pairs, so that Lust appears in connection with Avarice, and Anger with Pride. The four cardinal virtues opposed to them would be Chastity and Generosity, together with Gentleness and Humility.

When we compare these profound ideas of morality, as they are entertained by oriental nations, with the celebrated cardinal virtues of Plato, which have been recapitulated again and again— Justice, Valour, Temperance, and Wisdom—it is plain that the latter are not based on any clear, leading idea, but are chosen on grounds that are superficial and, in part, obviously false. Virtues must be qualities of the will, but Wisdom is chiefly an attribute of the Intellect. $\Sigma\omega\phi\rho\sigma\sigma\acute{\nu}\nu\eta$, which Cicero translates *Temperantia,* is a very indefinite and ambiguous word, and it admits, therefore, of a variety of applications: it may mean discretion, or abstinence, or keeping a level head. Courage is not a virtue at all; although

---

[1] Edit of 1819, vol. vi., p. 372.

sometimes it is a servant or instrument of virtue; but it is just as ready to become the servant of the greatest villainy. It is really a quality of temperament. Even Geulinx (in the preface to his *Ethics)* condemned the Platonic virtues and put the following in their place: Diligence, Obedience, Justice and Humility; which are obviously bad. The Chinese distinguish five cardinal virtues: Sympathy, Justice, Propriety, Wisdom, and Sincerity. The virtues of Christianity are theological, not cardinal: Faith, Love, and Hope.

Fundamental disposition towards others, assuming the character either of Envy or of Sympathy, is the point at which the moral virtues and vices of mankind first diverge. These two diametrically opposite qualities exist in every man; for they spring from the inevitable comparison which he draws between his own lot and that of others. According as the result of this comparison affects his individual character does the one or the other of these qualities become the source and principle of all his action. Envy builds the wall between *Thee* and *Me* thicker and stronger; Sympathy makes it slight and transparent; nay, sometimes it pulls down the wall altogether; and then the distinction between self and not-self vanishes.

Valour, which has been mentioned as a virtue, or rather the Courage on which it is based (for valour is only courage in war), deserves a closer examination. The ancients reckoned Courage among the virtues, and cowardice among the vices; but there is no corresponding idea in the Christian scheme, which makes for charity and patience, and in its teaching forbids all enmity or even resistance. The result is that with the moderns Courage is no longer a virtue. Nevertheless it must be admitted that cowardice does not seem to be very compatible with any nobility of character—if only for the reason that it betrays an overgreat apprehension about one's own person.

Courage, however, may also be explained as a readiness to meet ills that threaten at the moment, in order to avoid greater ills that lie in the future; whereas cowardice does the contrary. But this readiness is of the same quality as *patience,* for patience consists in the clear consciousness that there greater evils than those which are present, and that any violent attempt to flee from or guard against the ills we have may bring the others upon us. Courage, then, would be a kind of patience; and since it is patience that enables us to practise forbearance and self-control, Courage is, through the medium of patience, at least akin to virtue.

But perhaps Courage admits of being considered from a higher point of view. The fear of death may in every case be traced to a deficiency in that natural philosophy—natural, and therefore resting on mere feeling—which gives a man the assurance that he exists in everything outside him just as much as in his own person; so that the death of his person can do him little harm. But it is just this very assurance that would give a man heroic Courage; and therefore, as the reader will recollect from my *Ethics,* Courage comes from the same source as the virtues of Justice and Humanity. This is, I admit, to take a very high view of the matter; but apart from it I cannot well explain why cowardice seems contemptible, and personal Courage a noble and sublime thing; for no lower point of view enables me to see why a finite individual who is everything to himself—nay, who is himself even the very fundamental condition of the existence of the rest of the world—should not put his own preservation above every other aim. It is, then, an insufficient explanation of Courage to make it rest only on utility, to give it an empirical and not a transcendental character. It may have been for some such reason that Calderon once uttered a sceptical but remarkable opinion in regard to Courage, nay, actually denied its reality; and put his denial into the mouth of a wise old minister, addressing his young sovereign. "Although," he observed, "natural fear is operative in all alike, a man may be brave in not letting it be seen; and it is this that constitutes Courage":—

> *Que aunque el natural temor*
> *En todos obra igualmente,*
> *No mostrarle es ser valiente*
> *Y esto es lo que hace el valor.*[1]

In regard to the difference which I have mentioned between the ancients and the moderns in their estimate of Courage as a virtue, it must be remembered that by Virtue, *virtus,* ἀρετή the ancients understood every excellence or quality that was praise-

---

[1] *La Hija del Aire,* ii., 2.

worthy in itself, it might be moral or intellectual, or possibly only physical. But when Christianity demonstrated that the fundamental tendency of life was moral, it was moral superiority alone that henceforth attached to the notion of Virtue. Meanwhile the earlier usage still survived in the elder Latinists, and also in Italian writers, as is proved by the well-known meaning of the word *virtuoso*. The special attention of students should be drawn to this wider range of the idea of Virtue amongst the ancients, as otherwise it might easily be a source of secret perplexity. I may recommend two passages preserved for us by Stobæus, which will serve this purpose. One of them is apparently from the Pythagorean philosopher Metopos, in which the fitness of every bodily member is declared to be a virtue. The other pronounces that the virtue of a shoemaker is to make good shoes. This may also serve to explain why it is that in the ancient scheme of ethics virtues and vices are mentioned which find no place in ours.

As the place of Courage amongst the virtues is a matter of doubt, so is that of Avarice amongst the vices. It must not, however, be confounded with greed, which is the most immediate meaning of the Latin word *avaritia*. Let us then draw up and examine the arguments *pro et contra* in regard to Avarice, and leave the final judgment to be formed by every man for himself.

On the one hand it is argued that it is not Avarice which is a vice, but extravagance, its opposite. Extravagance springs from a brutish limitation to the present moment, in comparison with which the future, existing as it does only in thought, is as nothing. It rests upon the illusion that sensual pleasures possess a positive or real value. Accordingly, future need and misery is the price at which the spendthrift purchases pleasures that are empty, fleeting, and often no more than imaginary; or else feeds his vain, stupid self-conceit on the bows and scrapes of parasites who laugh at him in secret, or on the gaze of the mob and those who envy his magnificence. We should, therefore, shun the spendthrift as though he had the plague, and on discovering his vice break with him betimes, in order that later on, when the consequences of his extravagance ensue, we may neither have to help to bear them, nor, on the other hand, have to play the part of the friends of Timon of Athens.

At the same time it is not to be expected that he who foolishly squanders his own fortune will leave another man's intact, if it should chance to be committed to his keeping; nay, *sui profusus* and *alieni appetens* are by Sallust very rightly conjoined. Hence it is that extravagance leads not only to impoverishment but also to crime; and crime amongst the moneyed classes is almost always the result of extravagance. It is accordingly with justice that the *Koran* declares all spendthrifts to be "brothers of Satan."

But it is superfluity that Avarice brings in its train, and when was superfluity ever unwelcome? That must be a good vice which has good consequences. Avarice proceeds upon the principle that all pleasure is only negative in its operation and that the happiness which consists of a series of pleasures is a chimaera; that, on the contrary, it is pains which are positive and extremely real. Accordingly, the avaricious man foregoes the former in order that he may be the better preserved from the latter, and thus it is that *bear and forbear*—*sustine et abstine*—is his maxim. And because he knows, further, how inexhaustible are the possibilities of misfortune, and how innumerable the paths of danger, he increases the means of avoiding them, in order, if possible, to surround himself with a triple wall of protection. Who, then, can say where precaution against disaster begins to be exaggerated? He alone who knows where the malignity of fate reaches its limit. And even if precaution were exaggerated it is an error which at the most would hurt the man who took it, and not others. If he will never need the treasures which he lays up for himself, they will one day benefit others whom nature has made less careful. That until then he withdraws the money from circulation is no misfortune; for money is not an article of consumption: it only represents the good things which a man may actually possess, and is not one itself. Coins are only counters; their value is what they represent; and what they represent cannot be withdrawn from circulation. Moreover, by holding back the money, the value of the remainder which is in circulation is enhanced by precisely the same amount. Even though it be the case, as is said, that many a miser comes in the end to love money itself for its own sake, it is equally certain that many a spendthrift, on the other hand, loves spending and squandering for no better

reason. Friendship with a miser is not only without danger, but it
is profitable, because of the great advantages it can bring. For it is
doubtless those who are nearest and dearest to the miser who on his
death will reap the fruits of the self-control which he exercised; but
even in his lifetime, too, something may be expected of him in cases
of great need. At any rate one can always hope for more from him
than from the spendthrift, who has lost his all and is himself helpless
and in debt. *Mas dà el duro que el desnudo,* says a Spanish proverb; the
man who has a hard heart will give more than the man who has an
empty purse. The upshot of all this is that Avarice is not a vice.

On the other side, it may be said that Avarice is the quintes-
sence of all vices. When physical pleasures seduce a man from the
right path, it is his sensual nature—the animal part of him—which
is at fault. He is carried away by its attractions, and, overcome
by the impression of the moment, he acts without thinking of
the consequences. When, on the other hand, he is brought by age
or bodily weakness to the condition in which the vices that he
could never abandon end by abandoning him, and his capacity
for physical pleasure dies—if he turns to Avarice, the intellectual
desire survives the sensual. Money, which represents all the good
things of this world, and is these good things in the abstract, now
becomes the dry trunk overgrown with all the dead lusts of the
flesh, which are egoism in the abstract. They come to life again
in the love of the Mammon. The transient pleasure of the senses
has become a deliberate and calculated lust of money, which, like
that to which it is directed, is symbolical in its nature, and, like it,
indestructible.

This obstinate love of the pleasures of the world—a love which,
as it were, outlives itself; this utterly incorrigible sin, this refined
and sublimated desire of the flesh, is the abstract form in which all
lusts are concentrated, and to which it stands like a general idea to
individual particulars. Accordingly, Avarice is the vice of age, just
as extravagance is the vice of youth.

This *disputatio in utramque partem*—this debate for and against—is
certainly calculated to drive us into accepting the *juste milieu*
morality of Aristotle; a conclusion what is also supported by the
following consideration.

Every human perfection is allied to a defect into which it threatens to pass; but it is also true that every defect is allied to a perfection. Hence it is that if, as often happens, we make a mistake about a man, it is because at the beginning of our acquaintance with him we confound his defects with the kinds of perfection to which they are allied. The cautious man seems to us a coward; the economical man, a miser; the spendthrift seems liberal; the rude fellow, downright and sincere; the foolhardy person looks as if he were going to work with a noble self-confidence; and so on in many other cases.

★ ★ ★ ★ ★

No one can live among men without feeling drawn again and again to the tempting supposition that moral baseness and intellectual incapacity are closely connected, as though they both sprang direct from one source. That that, however, is not so, I have shown in detail.[1] That it seems to be so is merely due to the fact that both are so often found together; and the circumstance is to be explained by the very frequent occurrence of each of them, so that it may easily happen for both to be compelled to live under one roof. At the same time it is not to be denied that they play into each other's hands to their mutual benefit; and it is this that produces the very unedifying spectacle which only too many men exhibit, and that makes the world to go as it goes. A man who is unintelligent is very likely to show his perfidy, villainy and malice; whereas a clever man understands better how to conceal these qualities. And how often, on the other hand, does a perversity of heart prevent a man from seeing truths which his intelligence is quite capable of grasping!

Nevertheless, let no one boast. Just as every man, though he be the greatest genius, has very definite limitations in some one sphere of knowledge, and thus attests his common origin with the essentially perverse and stupid mass of mankind, so also has every man something in his nature which is positively evil. Even the best, nay the noblest, character will sometimes surprise us by

---

[1] In my chief work, vol. ii., ch. xix.

isolated traits of depravity; as though it were to acknowledge his kinship with the human race, in which villainy—nay, cruelty—is to be found in that degree. For it was just in virtue of this evil in him, this bad principle, that of necessity he became a man. And for the same reason the world in general is what my clear mirror of it has shown it to be.

But in spite of all this the difference even between one man and another is incalculably great, and many a one would be horrified to see another as he really is. Oh for some Asmodeus of morality, to make not only roofs and walls transparent to his favourites, but also to lift the veil of dissimulation, fraud, hypocrisy, pretence, falsehood and deception, which is spread over all things! to show how little true honesty there is in the world, and how often, even where it is least to be expected, behind all the exterior outwork of virtue, secretly and in the innermost recesses, unrighteousness sits at the helm! It is just on this account that so many men of the better kind have four-footed friends: for, to be sure, how is a man to get relief from the endless dissimulation, falsity and malice of mankind, if there were no dogs into whose honest faces he can look without distrust?

For what is our civilised world but a big masquerade? where you meet knights, priests, soldiers, men of learning, barristers, clergymen, philosophers, and I don't know what all! But they are not what they pretend to be; they are only masks, and, as a rule, behind the masks you will find money-makers. One man, I suppose, puts on the mask of law, which he has borrowed for the purpose from a barrister, only in order to be able to give another man a sound drubbing; a second has chosen the mask of patriotism and the public welfare with a similar intent; a third takes religion or purity of doctrine. For all sorts of purposes men have often put on the mask of philosophy, and even of philanthropy, and I know not what besides. Women have a smaller choice. As a rule they avail themselves of the mask of morality, modesty, domesticity, and humility. Then there are general masks, without any particular character attaching to them, like dominoes. They may be met with everywhere; and of this sort is the strict rectitude, the courtesy, the sincere sympathy, the smiling friendship, that people profess. The whole of these masks as a rule are merely, as I have said, a disguise for some industry, commerce, or speculation. It is merchants alone who in this respect constitute any honest class. They are the only people who give themselves out to be what they are; and therefore they go about without any mask at all, and consequently take a humble rank.

It is very necessary that a man should be apprised early in life that it is a masquerade in which he finds himself. For otherwise there are many things which he will fail to understand and put up with, nay, at which he will be completely puzzled, and that man longest of all whose heart is made of better clay—

Et meliore luto finxit præcordia Titan.[1]

Such for instance is the favour that villainy finds; the neglect that merit, even the rarest and the greatest, suffers at the hands of those of the same profession; the hatred of truth and great capacity; the ignorance of scholars in their own province; and the fact that true wares are almost always despised and the merely specious ones in request. Therefore let even the young be instructed betimes that in this masquerade the apples are of wax, the flowers of silk, the fish of pasteboard, and that all things—yes, all things—are toys and trifles; and that of two men whom he may see earnestly engaged in business, one is supplying spurious goods and the other paying for them in false coin.

But there are more serious reflections to be made, and worse things to be recorded. Man is at bottom a savage, horrible beast. We know it, if only in the business of taming and restraining him which we call civilisation. Hence it is that we are terrified if now and then his nature breaks out. Wherever and whenever the locks and chains of law and order fall off and give place to anarchy, he shows himself for what he is. But it is unnecessary to wait for anarchy in order to gain enlightenment on this subject. A hundred records, old and new, produce the conviction that in his unrelenting cruelty man is in no way inferior to the tiger and the hyæna. A forcible example is supplied by a publication of the year 1841 entitled *Slavery and the Internal Slave Trade in the United States*

---

[1] Juvenal, *Sat.* 14, 34.

*of North America: being replies to questions transmitted by the British
Anti-slavery Society to the American Anti-slavery Society.*[1] This book
constitutes one of the heaviest indictments against the human
race. No one can put it down without a feeling of horror, and
few without tears. For whatever the reader may have ever heard,
or imagined, or dreamt, of the unhappy condition of slavery, or
indeed of human cruelty in general, it will seem small to him
when he reads of the way in which those devils in human form,
those bigoted, church-going, strictly Sabbatarian rascals—and in
particular the Anglican priests among them—treated their innocent black brothers, who by wrong and violence had got into
their diabolical clutches.

Other examples are furnished by Tschudi's *Travels in Peru,* in
the description which he gives of the treatment of the Peruvian
soldiers at the hands of their officers; and by Macleod's *Travels in
Eastern Africa,* where the author tells of the cold-blooded and truly
devilish cruelty with which the Portuguese in Mozambique treat
their slaves. But we need not go for examples to the New World,
that obverse side of our planet. In the year 1848 it was brought to
life that in England, not in one, but apparently in a hundred cases
within a brief period, a husband had poisoned his wife or *vice
versâ,* or both had joined in poisoning their children, or in tortur-
ing them slowly to death by starving and ill-treating them, with
no other object than to get the money for burying them which
they had insured in the Burial Clubs against their death. For this
purpose a child was often insured in several, even in as many as
twenty clubs at once.[2]

Details of this character belong, indeed, to the blackest pages
in the criminal records of humanity. But, when all is said, it is the
inward and innate character of man, this god *par excellence* of the
Pantheists, from which they and everything like them proceed.
In every man there dwells, first and foremost, a colossal egoism,

---

[1] *Translator's Note.* If Schopenhauer were writing to-day, he would with equal
truth point to the miseries of the African trade. I have slightly abridged this passage, as some of the evils against which he protested no longer exist.
[2] Cf. *The Times,* 20th, 22nd and 23rd Sept., 1848, and also 12th Dec., 1853.

which breaks the bounds of right and justice with the greatest freedom, as everyday life shows on a small scale, and as history on every page of it on a large. Does not the recognised need of a balance of power in Europe, with the anxious way in which it is preserved, demonstrate that man is a beast of prey, who no sooner sees a weaker man near him than he falls upon him without fail? and does not the same hold good of the affairs of ordinary life?

But to the boundless egoism of our nature there is joined more or less in every human breast a fund of hatred, anger, envy, rancour and malice, accumulated like the venom in a serpent's tooth, and waiting only for an opportunity of venting itself, and then, like a demon unchained, of storming and raging. If a man has no great occasion for breaking out, he will end by taking advantage of the smallest, and by working it up into something great by the aid of his imagination; for, however small it may be, it is enough to rouse his anger—

Quantulacunque adeo est occasio, sufficit irae[1]—

and then he will carry it as far as he can and may. We see this in daily life, where such outbursts are well known under the name of "venting one's gall on something." It will also have been observed that if such outbursts meet with no opposition the subject of them feels decidedly the better for them afterwards. That anger is not without its pleasure is a truth that was recorded even by Aristotle;[2] and he quotes a passage from Homer, who declares anger to be sweeter than honey. But not in anger alone—in hatred too, which stands to anger like a chronic to an acute disease, a man may indulge with the greatest delight:

> *Now hatred is by far the longest pleasure,*
> *Men love in haste, but they detest at leisure.*[3]

Gobineau in his work *Les Races Humaines* has called man *l'animal méchant par excellence.* People take this very ill, because they feel that it hits them; but he is quite right, for man is the

---

[1]Juvenal, *Sat.* 13, 183.
[2]*Rhet.,* i., 11; ii., 2.
[3]Byron, *Don Juan,* c. xiii. 6.

only animal which causes pain to others without any further purpose than just to cause it. Other animals never do it except to satisfy their hunger, or in the rage of combat. If it is said against the tiger that he kills more than eats, he strangles his prey only for the purpose of eating it; and if he cannot eat it, the only explanation is, as the French phrase has it, that *ses yeux sont plus grands que son estomac.* No animal ever torments another for the mere purpose of tormenting, but man does it, and it is this that constitutes the diabolical feature in his character which is so much worse than the merely animal. I have already spoken of the matter in its broad aspect; but it is manifest even in small things, and every reader has a daily opportunity of observing it. For instance, if two little dogs are playing together—and what a genial and charming sight it is—and a child of three or four years joins them, it is almost inevitable for it to begin hitting them with a whip or stick, and thereby show itself, even at that age, *l'animal méchant par excellence.* The love of teasing and playing tricks, which is common enough, may be traced to the same source. For instance, if a man has expressed his annoyance at any interruption or other petty inconvenience, there will be no lack of people who for that very reason will bring it about: *animal méchant par excellence!* This is so certain that a man should be careful not to express any annoyance at small evils. On the other hand he should also be careful not to express his pleasure at any trifle, for, if he does so, men will act like the gaoler who, when he found that his prisoner had performed the laborious task of taming a spider, and took a pleasure in watching it, immediately crushed it under his foot: *l'animal méchant par excellence!* This is why all animals are instinctively afraid of the sight, or even of the track of a man, that *animal méchant par excellence!* nor does their instinct play them false; for it is man alone who hunts game for which he has no use and which does him no harm.

It is a fact, then, that in the heart of every man there lies a wild beast which only waits for an opportunity to storm and rage, in its desire to inflict pain on others, or, if they stand in his way, to kill them. It is this which is the source of all the lust of war and battle. In trying to tame and to some extent hold it in check, the intelligence, its appointed keeper, has always enough to do. People may, if they please, call it the radical evil of human nature—a name which will at least serve those with whom a word stands for an explanation. I say, however, that it is the will to live, which, more and more embittered by the constant sufferings of existence, seeks to alleviate its own torment by causing torment in others. But in this way a man gradually develops in himself real cruelty and malice. The observation may also be added that as, according to Kant, matter subsists only through the antagonism of the powers of expansion and contraction, so human society subsists only by the antagonism of hatred, or anger, and fear. For there is a moment in the life of all of us when the malignity of our nature might perhaps make us murderers, if it were not accompanied by a due admixture of fear to keep it within bounds; and this fear, again, would make a man the sport and laughing stock of every boy, if anger were not lying ready in him, and keeping watch.

But it is *Schadenfreude,* a mischievous delight in the misfortunes of others, which remains the worst trait in human nature. It is a feeling which is closely akin to cruelty, and differs from it, to say the truth, only as theory from practice. In general, it may be said of it that it takes the place which pity ought to take—pity which is its opposite, and the true source of all real justice and charity.

Envy is also opposed to pity, but in another sense; envy, that is to say, is produced by a cause directly antagonistic to that which produces the delight in mischief. The opposition between pity and envy on the one hand, and pity and the delight in mischief on the other, rests, in the main, on the occasions which call them forth. In the case of envy it is only as a direct effect of the cause which excites it that we feel it at all. That is just the reason why envy, although it is a reprehensible feeling, still admits of some excuse, and is, in general, a very human quality; whereas the delight in mischief is diabolical, and its taunts are the laughter of hell.

The delight in mischief, as I have said, takes the place which pity ought to take. Envy, on the contrary, finds a place only where there is no inducement to pity, or rather an inducement to its opposite; and it is just as this opposite that envy arises in the human breast; and so far, therefore, it may still be reckoned a human sentiment. Nay, I am afraid that no one will be found to be entirely free from it. For that a man should feel his own lack of things more bitterly at the sight of another's delight in the enjoyment of them, is natural; nay, it is inevitable; but this should not rouse his hatred of the man who is happier than himself. It is just this hatred, however, in which true envy consists. Least of all should a man be envious, when it is a question, not of the gifts of fortune, or chance, or another's favour, but of the gifts of nature; because everything that is innate in a man rests on a metaphysical basis, and possesses justification of a higher kind; it is, so to speak, given him by Divine grace. But, unhappily, it is just in the case of personal advantages that envy is most irreconcilable. Thus it is that intelligence, or even genius, cannot get on in the world without begging pardon for its existence, wherever it is not in a position to be able, proudly and boldly, to despise the world.

In other words, if envy is aroused only by wealth, rank, or power, it is often kept down by egoism, which perceives that, on occasion, assistance, enjoyment, support, protection, advancement, and so on, may be hoped for from the object of envy, or that at least by intercourse with him a man may himself win honour from the reflected light of his superiority; and here, too, there is the hope of one day attaining all those advantages himself. On the other hand, in the envy that is directed to natural gifts and personal advantages, like beauty in women, or intelligence in men, there is no consolation or hope of one kind or the other; so that nothing remains but to indulge a bitter and irreconcilable hatred of the person who possesses these privileges; and hence the only remaining desire is to take vengeance on him.

But here the envious man finds himself in an unfortunate position; for all his blows fall powerless as soon as it is known that they come from him. Accordingly he hides his feelings as carefully as if they were secret sins, and so becomes an inexhaustible inventor of tricks and artifices and devices for concealing and masking his procedure, in order that, unperceived, he may wound the object of his envy. For instance, with an air of the utmost unconcern he will ignore the advantages which are eating his heart out; he will neither see them, nor know them, nor have observed or even heard of them, and thus make himself a master in the art of dissimulation. With great cunning he will completely overlook the man whose brilliant qualities are gnawing at his heart, and act as though he were quite an unimportant person; he will take no notice of him, and, on occasion, will have even quite forgotten his existence. But at the same time he will before all things endeavour by secret machination carefully to deprive those advantages of any opportunity of showing themselves and becoming known. Then out of his dark corner he will attack these qualities with censure, mockery, ridicule and calumny, like the toad which spurts its poison from a hole. No less will he enthusiastically praise unimportant people, or even indifferent or bad performances in the same sphere. In short, he will become a Proteas in stratagem, in order to wound others without showing himself. But what is the use of it? The trained eye recognises him in spite of it all. He betrays himself, if by nothing else, by the way in which he timidly avoids and flies from the object of his envy, who stands the more completely alone, the more brilliant he is; and this is the reason why pretty girls have no friends of their own sex. He betrays himself, too, by the causeless hatred which he shows—a hatred which finds vent in a violent explosion at any circumstance however trivial, though it is often only the product of his imagination. How many such men there are in the world may be recognised by the universal praise of modesty, that is, of a virtue invented on behalf of dull and commonplace people. Nevertheless, it is a virtue which, by exhibiting the necessity for dealing considerately with the wretched plight of these people, is just what calls attention to it.

For our self-consciousness and our pride there can be nothing more flattering than the sight of envy lurking in its retreat and plotting its schemes; but never let a man forget that where there is envy there is hatred, and let him be careful not to make a false friend out of any envious person. Therefore it is important to our safety to lay envy bare; and a man should study to discover its tricks, as it is everywhere to be found and always goes about

incognito; or as I have said, like a venomous toad it lurks in dark
corners. It deserves neither quarter nor sympathy; but as we can
never reconcile it let our rule of conduct be to scorn it with a
good heart, and as our happiness and glory is torture to it we may
rejoice in its sufferings:—

> *Den Neid wirst nimmer du versöhnen;*
> *So magst du ihn getrost verhöhnen.*
> *Dein Glück, dein Ruhm ist ihm ein Leiden:*
> *Magst drum an seiner Quaal dich weiden.*

We have been taking a look at the *depravity* of man, and it is a
sight which may well fill us with horror. But now we must cast
our eyes on the *misery* of his existence; and when we have done
so, and are horrified by that too, we must look back again at his
depravity. We shall then find that they hold the balance to each
other. We shall perceive the eternal justice of things; for we shall
recognise that the world is itself the Last Judgment on it, and
we shall begin to understand why it is that everything that lives
must pay the penalty of its existence, first in living and then in
dying. Thus the evil of the penalty accords with the evil of the
sin—*malum pœnæ* with *malum culpæ.* From the same point of view
we lose our indignation at that intellectual incapacity of the great
majority of mankind which in life so often disgusts us. In this
Sansara, as the Buddhists call it, human misery, human depravity
and human folly correspond with one another perfectly, and they
are of like magnitude. But if, on some special inducement, we
direct our gaze to one of them, and survey it in particular, it seems
to exceed the other two. This, however, is an illusion, and merely
the effect of their colossal range.

All things proclaim this *Sansara;* more than all else, the world
of mankind; in which, from a moral point of view, villainy and
baseness, and from an intellectual point of view, incapacity and
stupidity, prevail to a horrifying extent. Nevertheless, there appear
in it, although very spasmodically, and always as a fresh surprise,
manifestations of honesty, of goodness, nay, even of nobility; and
also of great intelligence, of the thinking mind, of genius. They
never quite vanish, but like single points of light gleam upon us out

of the great dark mass. We must accept them as a pledge that this *Sansara* contains a good and redeeming principle, which is capable of breaking through and of filling and freeing the whole of it.

★ ★ ★ ★ ★

The readers of my *Ethics* know that with me the ultimate foundation of morality is the truth which in the *Vedas* and the *Vedanta* receives its expression in the established, mystical formula, *Tat twam asi (This is thyself)*, which is spoken with reference to every living thing, be it man or beast, and is called the *Mahavakya,* the great word.

Actions which proceed in accordance with this principle, such as those of the philanthropist, may indeed be regarded as the beginning of mysticism. Every benefit rendered with a pure intention proclaims that the man who exercises it acts in direct conflict with the world of appearance; for he recognises himself as identical with another individual, who exists in complete separation from him. Accordingly, all disinterested kindness is inexplicable; it is a mystery; and hence in order to explain it a man has to resort to all sorts of fictions. When Kant had demolished all other arguments for theism, he admitted one only, that it gave the best interpretation and solution of such mysterious actions, and of all others like them. He therefore allowed it to stand as a presumption unsusceptible indeed of theoretical proof, but valid from a practical point of view. I may, however, express my doubts whether he was quite serious about it. For to make morality rest on theism is really to reduce morality to egoism; although the English, it is true, as also the lowest classes of society with us, do not perceive the possibility of any other foundation for it.

The above-mentioned recognition of a man's own true being in another individual objectively presented to him, is exhibited in a particularly beautiful and clear way in the cases in which a man, already destined to death beyond any hope of rescue, gives himself up to the welfare of others with great solicitude and zeal, and tries to save them. Of this kind is the well-known story of a servant who was bitten in a courtyard at night by a mad dog. In the belief that she was beyond hope, she seized the dog and dragged it into a stable, which she then locked, so that no one else might be bitten. Then again there is the incident in Naples, which Tischbein has immortalised in one of his *aquarelles.* A son, fleeing from the lava which is rapidly streaming towards the sea, is carrying his aged father on his back. When there is only a narrow strip of land left between the devouring elements, the father bids the son put him down, so that the son may save himself by flight, as otherwise both will be lost. The son obeys, and as he goes casts a glance of farewell on his father. This is the moment depicted. The historical circumstance which Scott represents in his masterly way in *The Heart of Midlothian,* chap, ii., is of a precisely similar kind; where, of two delinquents condemned to death, the one who by his awkwardness caused the capture of the other happily sets him free in the chapel by overpowering the guard after the execution-sermon, without at the same time making any attempt on his own behalf. Nay, in the same category must also be placed the scene which is represented in a common engraving, which may perhaps be objectionable to western readers—I mean the one in which a soldier, kneeling to be shot, is trying by waving a cloth to frighten away his dog who wants to come to him.

In all these cases we see an individual in the face of his own immediate and certain destruction no longer thinking of saving himself, so that he may direct the whole of his efforts to saving some one else. How could there be a clearer expression of the consciousness that what is being destroyed is only a phenomenon, and that the destruction itself is only a phenomenon; that, on the other hand, the real being of the man who meets his death is untouched by that event, and lives on in the other man, in whom even now, as his action betrays, he so clearly perceives it to exist? For if this were not so, and it was his real being which was about to be annihilated, how could that being spend its last efforts in showing such an ardent sympathy in the welfare and continued existence of another?

There are two different ways in which a man may become conscious of his own existence. On the one hand, he may have an empirical perception of it, as it manifests itself externally—something so small that it approaches vanishing point; set in a

world which, as regards time and space, is infinite; one only of
the thousand millions of human creatures who run about on this
planet for a very brief period and are renewed every thirty years.
On the other hand, by going down into the depths of his own
nature, a man may become conscious that he is all in all; that,
in fact, he is the only real being; and that, in addition, this real
being perceives itself again in others, who present themselves from
without, as though they formed a mirror of himself.

Of these two ways in which a man may come to know what he
is, the first grasps the phenomenon alone, the mere product of *the
principle of individuation;* whereas the second makes a man immediately conscious that he is *the thing-in-itself.* This is a doctrine in
which, as regards the first way, I have Kant, and as regards both, I
have the *Vedas,* to support me.

There is, it is true, a simple objection to the second method. It
may be said to assume that one and the same being can exist in
different places at the same time, and yet be complete in each of
them. Although, from an empirical point of view, this is the most
palpable impossibility—nay, absurdity—it is nevertheless perfectly
true of the thing-in-itself. The impossibility and the absurdity of it,
empirically, are only due to the forms which phenomena assume,
in accordance with the principle of individuation. For the thing-
in-itself, the will to live, exists whole and undivided in every being,
even in the smallest, as completely as in the sum-total of all things
that ever were or are or will be. This is why every being, even the
smallest, says to itself, So long as I am safe, let the world perish—
dum ego salvus sim, pereat mundus. And, in truth, even if only one
individual were left in the world, and all the rest were to perish,
the one that remained would still possess the whole self-being of
the world, uninjured and undiminished, and would laugh at the
destruction of the world as an illusion. This conclusion *per impossible* may be balanced by the counter-conclusion, which is on all
fours with it, that if that last individual were to be annihilated in
and with him the whole world would be destroyed. It was in this
sense that the mystic Angelas Silesius[1] declared that God could

---

[1] *Translator's Note.* Angelus Silesius, see *Counsels and Maxims,* p. 39, note.

not live for a moment without him, and that if he were to be annihilated God must of necessity give up the ghost:—

> *Ich weiss dass ohne mich Gott nicht ein Nu kann leben;*
> *Werd' ich zunicht, er muss von Noth den Geist aufgeben.*

But the empirical point of view also to some extent enables us to perceive that it is true, or at least possible, that our self can exist in other beings whose consciousness is separated and different from our own. That this is so is shown by the experience of somnambulists. Although the identity of their ego is preserved throughout, they know nothing, when they awake, of all that a moment before they themselves said, did or suffered. So entirely is the individual consciousness a phenomenon that even in the same ego two consciousnesses can arise of which the one knows nothing of the other.

Government

It is a characteristic failing of the Germans to look in the clouds for what lies at their feet. An excellent example of this is furnished by the treatment which the idea of *Natural Right* has received at the hands of professors of philosophy. When they are called upon to explain those simple relations of human life which make up the substance of this right, such as Right and Wrong, Property, State, Punishment and so on, they have recourse to the most extravagant, abstract, remote and meaningless conceptions, and out of them build a Tower of Babel reaching to the clouds, and taking this or that form according to the special whim of the professor for the time being. The clearest and simplest relations of life, such as affect us directly, are thus made quite unintelligible, to the great detriment of the young people who are educated in such a school. These relations themselves are perfectly simple and easily understood—as the reader may convince himself if he will turn to the account which I have given of them in the *Foundation of Morality,* § 17, and in my chief work, bk. i., § 62. But at the sound of certain words, like Right, Freedom, the Good, Being—this nugatory infinitive of the copula—and many others of the same sort, the German's head begins to swim, and falling straightway into a kind of delirium he launches forth into high-flown phrases which have no meaning whatever. He takes the most remote and empty conceptions, and strings them together artificially, instead of fixing his eyes on the facts, and looking at things and relations as they really are. It is these things and relations which supply the ideas of Right and Freedom, and give them the only true meaning that they possess.

The man who starts from the preconceived opinion that the conception of Right must be a positive one, and then attempts to define it, will fail; for he is trying to grasp a shadow, to pursue a spectre, to search for what does not exist. The conception of Right is a negative one, like the conception of Freedom; its content is mere negation. It is the conception of Wrong which is positive; Wrong has the same significance as *injury—læsio*—in the widest sense of the term. An injury may be done either to a man's person or to his property or to his honour; and accordingly a man's rights are easy to define: every one has a right to do anything that injures no one else.

To have a right to do or claim a thing means nothing more than to be able to do or take or use it without thereby injuring any one else. *Simplex sigillum veri.* This definition shows how senseless many questions are; for instance, the question whether we have the right to take our own life. As far as concerns the personal claims which others may possibly have upon us, they are subject to the condition that we are alive, and fall to the ground when we die. To demand of a man, who does not care to live any longer for himself, that he should live on as a mere machine for the advantage of others is an extravagant pretension.

Although men's powers differ, their rights are alike. Their rights do not rest upon their powers, because Right is of a moral complexion; they rest on the fact that the same will to live shows itself in every man at the same stage of its manifestation. This, however, only applies to that original and abstract Right, which a man possesses as a man. The property, and also the honour, which a man acquires for himself by the exercise of his powers, depend on the measure and kind of power which he possesses, and so lend his Right a wider sphere of application. Here, then, equality comes to an end. The man who is better equipped, or more active, increases by adding to his gains, not his Right, but the number of the things to which it extends.

In my chief work[1] I have proved that the State in its essence is merely an institution existing for the purpose of protecting its members against outward attack or inward dissension. It follows from this that the ultimate ground on which the State is necessary is the acknowledged lack of Right in the human race. If Right were there, no one would think of a State; for no one would

---

[1] Bk. ii., ch. xlvii.

have any fear that his rights would be impaired; and a mere union against the attacks of wild beasts or the elements would have very little analogy with what we mean by a State. From this point of view it is easy to see how dull and stupid are the philosophasters who in pompous phrases represent that the State is the supreme end and flower of human existence. Such a view is the apotheosis of Philistinism.

If it were Right that ruled in the world, a man would have done enough in building his house, and would need no other protection than the right of possessing it, which would be obvious. But since Wrong is the order of the day, it is requisite that the man who has built his house should also be able to protect it. Otherwise his Right is *de facto* incomplete; the aggressor, that is to say, has the right of might—*Faustrecht;* and this is just the conception of Right which Spinoza entertains. He recognises no other. His words are: *unusquisque tantum juris habet quantum potentia valet;*[1] each man has as much right as he has power. And again: *uniuscujusque jus potentia ejus definitur;* each man's right is determined by his power.[2] Hobbes seems to have started this conception of Right,[3] and he adds the strange comment that the Right of the good Lord to all things rests on nothing but His omnipotence.

Now this is a conception of Right which, both in theory and in practice, no longer prevails in the civic world; but in the world in general, though abolished in theory, it continues to apply in practice. The consequences of neglecting it may be seen in the case of China. Threatened by rebellion within and foes without, this great empire is in a defenceless state, and has to pay the penalty of having cultivated only the arts of peace and ignored the arts of war.

There is a certain analogy between the operations of nature and those of man which is a peculiar but not fortuitous character, and is based on the identity of the will in both. When the herbivorous animals had taken their place in the organic world, beasts of prey made their appearance—necessarily a late appearance—in each

---

[1] *Tract. Theol. Pol.,* ch. ii., § 8.
[2] *Ethics,* IV., xxxvii., 1.
[3] Particularly in a passage in the *De Cive,* I, § 14.

species, and proceeded to live upon them. Just in the same way, as soon as by honest toil and in the sweat of their faces men have won from the ground what is needed for the support of their societies, a number of individuals are sure to arise in some of these societies, who, instead of cultivating the earth and living on its produce, prefer to take their lives in their hands and risk health and freedom by falling upon those who are in possession of what they have honestly earned, and by appropriating the fruits of their labour. These are the beasts of prey in the human race; they are the conquering peoples whom we find everywhere in history, from the most ancient to the most recent times. Their varying fortunes, as at one moment they succeed and at another fail, make up the general elements of the history of the world. Hence Voltaire was perfectly right when he said that the aim of all war is robbery. That those who engage in it are ashamed of their doings is clear by the fact that governments loudly protest their reluctance to appeal to arms except for purposes of self-defence. Instead of trying to excuse themselves by telling public and official lies, which are almost more revolting than war itself, they should take their stand, as bold as brass, on Macchiavelli's doctrine. The gist of it may be stated to be this: that whereas between one individual and another, and so far as concerns the law and morality of their relations, the principle, *Don't do to others what you wouldn't like done to yourself*, certainly applies, it is the converse of this principle which is appropriate in the case of nations and in politics: *What you wouldn't like done to yourself do to others.* If you do not want to be put under a foreign yoke, take time by the forelock, and put your neighbour under it himself; whenever, that is to say, his weakness offers you the opportunity. For if you let the opportunity pass, it will desert one day to the enemy's camp and offer itself there. Then your enemy will put you under his yoke; and your failure to grasp the opportunity may be paid for, not by the generation which was guilty of it, but by the next. This Macchiavellian principle is always a much more decent cloak for the lust of robbery than the rags of very obvious lies in a speech from the head of the State; lies, too, of a description which recalls the well-known story of the rabbit attacking the dog. Every State looks upon its neighbours as at bottom a horde of robbers, who will fall upon it as soon as they have the opportunity.

★ ★ ★ ★ ★

Between the serf, the farmer, the tenant, and the mortgagee, the difference is rather one of form than of substance. Whether the peasant belongs to me, or the land on which he has to get a living; whether the bird is mine, or its food, the tree or its fruit, is a matter of little moment; for, as Shakespeare makes Shylock say:—

> *You take my life*
> *When you do take the means whereby I live.*

The free peasant has, indeed, the advantage that he can go off and seek his fortune in the wide world; whereas the serf who is attached to the soil, *glebæ adscriptus,* has an advantage which is perhaps still greater, that when failure of crops or illness, old age or incapacity, render him helpless, his master must look after him, and so he sleeps well at night; whereas, if the crops fail, his master tosses about on his bed trying to think how he is to procure bread for his men. As long ago as Menander it was said that it is better to be the slave of a good master than to live miserably as a freeman. Another advantage possessed by the free is that if they have any talents they can improve their position; but the same advantage is not wholly withheld from the slave. If he proves himself useful to his master by the exercise of any skill, he is treated accordingly; just as in ancient Rome mechanics, foremen of workshops, architects, nay, even doctors, were generally slaves.

Slavery and poverty, then, are only two forms, I might almost say only two names, of the same thing, the essence of which is that a man's physical powers are employed, in the main, not for himself but for others; and this leads partly to his being over-loaded with work, and partly to his getting a scanty satisfaction for his needs. For Nature has given a man only as much physical power as will suffice, if he exerts it in moderation, to gain a sustenance from the earth. No great superfluity of power is his. If, then, a not inconsiderable number of men are relieved from the common burden of sustaining the existence of the human race, the burden of the

remainder is augmented, and they suffer. This is the chief source
of the evil which under the name of slavery, or under the name
of the proletariat, has always oppressed the great majority of the
human race.

But the more remote cause of it is luxury. In order, it may be said,
that some few persons may have what is unnecessary, superfluous,
and the product of refinement—nay, in order that they may satisfy
artificial needs—a great part of the existing powers of mankind
has to be devoted to this object, and therefore withdrawn from
the production of what is necessary and indispensable. Instead of
building cottages for themselves, thousands of men build mansions
for a few. Instead of weaving coarse materials for themselves and
their families, they make fine cloths, silk, or even lace, for the rich,
and in general manufacture a thousand objects of luxury for their
pleasure. A great part of the urban population consists of workmen
who make these articles of luxury; and for them and those who
give them work the peasants have to plough and sow and look
after the flocks as well as for themselves, and thus have more labour
than Nature originally imposed upon them. Moreover, the urban
population devotes a great deal of physical strength, and a great
deal of land, to such things as wine, silk, tobacco, hops, aspara-
gus and so on, instead of to corn, potatoes and cattle-breeding.
Further, a number of men are withdrawn from agriculture and
employed in ship-building and seafaring, in order that sugar, cof-
fee, tea and other goods may be imported. In short, a large part of
the powers of the human race is taken away from the production
of what is necessary, in order to bring what is superfluous and
unnecessary within the reach of a few. As long therefore as luxury
exists, there must be a corresponding amount of over-work and
misery, whether it takes the name of poverty or of slavery. The
fundamental difference between the two is that slavery originates
in violence, and poverty in craft. The whole unnatural condition
of society—the universal struggle to escape from misery, the sea-
trade attended with so much loss of life, the complicated interests
of commerce, and finally the wars to which it all gives rise—is due,
only and alone, to luxury, which gives no happiness even to those
who enjoy it, nay, makes them ill and bad-tempered. Accordingly

it looks as if the most effective way of alleviating human misery would be to diminish luxury, or even abolish it altogether.

There is unquestionably much truth in this train of thought. But the conclusion at which it arrives is refuted by an argument possessing this advantage over it—that it is confirmed by the testimony of experience. A certain amount of work is devoted to purposes of luxury. What the human race loses in this way in the *muscular power* which would otherwise be available for the necessities of existence is gradually made up to it a thousandfold by the *nervous power,* which, in a chemical sense, is thereby released. And since the intelligence and sensibility which are thus promoted are on a higher level than the muscular irritability which they supplant, so the achievements of mind exceed those of the body a thousandfold. One wise counsel is worth the work of many hands:—

Ὡς ἐν σόφον βουλεύμα τὰς πόλλων χείρας νικᾷ.

A nation of nothing but peasants would do little in the way of discovery and invention; but idle hands make active heads. Science and the Arts are themselves the children of luxury, and they discharge their debt to it. The work which they do is to perfect technology in all its branches, mechanical, chemical and physical; an art which in our days has brought machinery to a pitch never dreamt of before, and in particular has, by steam and electricity, accomplished things the like of which would, in earlier ages, have been ascribed to the agency of the devil. In manufactures of all kinds, and to some extent in agriculture, machines now do a thousand times more than could ever have been done by the hands of all the well-to-do, educated, and professional classes, and could ever have been attained if all luxury had been abolished and every one had returned to the life of a peasant. It is by no means the rich alone, but all classes, who derive benefit from these industries. Things which in former days hardly any one could afford are now cheap and abundant, and even the lowest classes are much better off in point of comfort. In the Middle Ages a King of England once borrowed a pair of silk stockings from one of his lords, so that he might wear them in giving an audience to the French ambassador. Even Queen Elizabeth was greatly pleased and astonished to receive a pair as a New Year's present; to-day every shopman has them. Fifty years ago ladies wore the kind of calico gowns which servants wear now. If mechanical science continues to progress at the same rate for any length of time, it may end by saving human labour almost entirely, just as horses are even now being largely superseded by machines. For it is possible to conceive that intellectual culture might in some degree become general in the human race; and this would be impossible as long as bodily labour was incumbent on any great part of it. Muscular irritability and nervous sensibility are always and everywhere, both generally and particularly, in antagonism; for the simple reason that it is one and the same vital power which underlies both. Further, since the arts have a softening effect on character, it is possible that quarrels great and small, wars and duels, will vanish from the world; just as both have become much rarer occurrences. However, it is not my object here to write a *Utopia*.

But apart from all this the arguments used above in favour of the abolition of luxury and the uniform distribution of all bodily labour are open to the objection that the great mass of mankind, always and everywhere, cannot do without leaders, guides and counsellors, in one shape or another, according to the matter in question; judges, governors, generals, officials, priests, doctors, men of learning, philosophers, and so on, are all a necessity. Their common task is to lead the race, for the greater part so incapable and perverse, through the labyrinth of life, of which each of them according to his position and capacity has obtained a general view, be his range wide or narrow. That these guides of the race should be permanently relieved of all bodily labour as well as of all vulgar need and discomfort; nay, that in proportion to their much greater achievements they should necessarily own and enjoy more than the common man, is natural and reasonable. Great merchants should also be included in the same privileged class, whenever they make far-sighted preparations for national needs.

★ ★ ★ ★ ★

The question of the sovereignty of the people is at bottom the same as the question whether any man can have an original right to rule a people against its will. How that proposition can be reasonably maintained I do not see. The people, it must be admitted, is sovereign; but it is a sovereign who is always a minor. It must have permanent guardians, and it can never exercise its rights itself, without creating dangers of which no one can foresee the end; especially as like all minors, it is very apt to become the sport of designing sharpers, in the shape of what are called demagogues.

Voltaire remarks that the first man to become a king was a successful soldier. It is certainly the case that all princes were originally victorious leaders of armies, and for a long time it was as such that they bore sway. On the rise of standing armies princes began to regard their people as a means of sustaining themselves and their soldiers, and treated them, accordingly, as though they were a herd of cattle, which had to be tended in order that it might provide wool, milk, and meat. The why and wherefore of all this, as I shall presently show in detail, is the fact that originally it was not right, but might, that ruled in the world. Might has the advantage of having been the first in the field. That is why it is impossible to do away with it and abolish it altogether; it must always have its place; and all that a man can wish or ask is that it should be found on the side of right and associated with it. Accordingly says the prince to his subjects: "I rule you in virtue of the power which I possess. But, on the other hand, it excludes that of any one else, and I shall suffer none but my own, whether it comes from without, or arises within by one of you trying to oppress another. In this way, then, you are protected." The arrangement was carried out; and just because it was carried out the old idea of kingship developed with time and progress into quite a different idea, and put the other one in the background, where it may still be seen, now and then, flitting about like a spectre. Its place has been taken by the idea of the king as father of his people, as the firm and unshakable pillar which alone supports and maintains the whole organisation of law and order, and consequently the rights of every man.[1]

---

[1] We read in Stobæus, *Florilegium,* ch. xliv., 41, of a Persian custom, by which, whenever a king died, there was a five days' anarchy, in order that people might perceive the advantage of having kings and laws.

But a king can accomplish this only by inborn prerogative which reserves authority to him and to him alone—an authority which is supreme, indubitable, and beyond all attack, nay, to which every one renders instinctive obedience. Hence the king is rightly said to rule "by the grace of God." He is always the most useful person in the State, and his services are never too dearly repaid by any Civil List, however heavy.

But even as late a writer as Macchiavelli was so decidedly imbued with the earlier or mediæval conception of the position of a prince that he treats it as a matter which is self-evident: he never discusses it, but tacitly takes it as the presupposition and basis of his advice. It may be said generally that his book is merely the theoretical statement and consistent and systematic exposition of the practice prevailing in his time. It is the novel statement of it in a complete theoretical form that lends it such a poignant interest. The same thing, I may remark in passing, applies to the immortal little work of La Rochefaucauld, who, however, takes private and not public life for his theme, and offers, not advice, but observations. The title of this fine little book is open, perhaps, to some objection: the contents are not, as a rule, either *maxims* or *reflections,* but *aperçus;* and that is what they should be called. There is much, too, in Macchiavelli that will be found also to apply to private life.

★ ★ ★ ★ ★

Right in itself is powerless; in nature it is Might that rules. To enlist might on the side of right, so that by means of it right may rule, is the problem of statesmanship. And it is indeed a hard problem, as will be obvious if we remember that almost every human breast is the seat of an egoism which has no limits, and is usually associated with an accumulated store of hatred and malice; so that at the very start feelings of enmity largely prevail over those of friendship. We have also to bear in mind that it is many millions of individuals so constituted who have to be kept in the bonds of law and order, peace and tranquillity; whereas originally every one had a right to say to every one else: *I am just as good as you are!* A consideration of all this must fill us with surprise that on the whole the world pursues its way so peacefully and quietly, and with so much law and order as we see to exist. It is the machinery of State which alone accomplishes it. For it is physical power alone which has any direct action on men; constituted as they generally are, it is for physical power alone that they have any feeling or respect.

If a man would convince himself by experience that this is the case, he need do nothing but remove all compulsion from his fellows, and try to govern them by clearly and forcibly representing to them what is reasonable, right, and fair, though at the same time it may be contrary to their interests. He would be laughed to scorn; and as things go that is the only answer he would get. It would soon be obvious to him that moral force alone is powerless. It is, then, physical force alone which is capable of securing respect. Now this force ultimately resides in the masses, where it is associated with ignorance, stupidity and injustice. Accordingly the main aim of statesmanship in these difficult circumstances is to put physical force in subjection to mental force—to intellectual superiority, and thus to make it serviceable. But if this aim is not itself accompanied by justice and good intentions the result of the business, if it succeeds, is that the State so erected consists of knaves and fools, the deceivers and the deceived. That this is the case is made gradually evident by the progress of intelligence amongst the masses, however much it may be repressed; and it leads to revolution. But if, contrarily, intelligence is accompanied by justice and good intentions, there arises a State as perfect as the character of human affairs will allow. It is very much to the purpose if justice and good intentions not only exist, but are also demonstrable and openly exhibited, and can be called to account publicly, and be subject to control. Care must be taken, however, lest the resulting participation of many persons in the work of government should affect the unity of the State, and inflict a loss of strength and concentration on the power by which its home and foreign affairs have to be administered. This is what almost always happens in republics. To produce a constitution which should satisfy all these demands would accordingly be the highest aim of statesmanship. But, as a matter of fact, statesmanship has to consider other things as well. It has to reckon with the people as they exist, and their national peculiarities. This is the raw material on which it has to work, and the ingredients of that material will always exercise a great effect on the completed scheme.

Statesmanship will have achieved a good deal if it so far attains its object as to reduce wrong and injustice in the community to a minimum. To banish them altogether, and to leave no trace of them, is merely the ideal to be aimed at; and it is only approximately that it can be reached. If they disappear in one direction, they creep in again in another; for wrong and injustice lie deeply rooted in human nature. Attempts have been made to attain the desired aim by artificial constitutions and systematic codes of law; but they are not in complete touch with the facts—they remain an asymptote, for the simple reason that hard and fast conceptions never embrace all possible cases, and cannot be made to meet individual instances. Such conceptions resemble the stones of a mosaic rather than the delicate shading in a picture. Nay, more: all experiments in this matter are attended with danger; because the material in question, namely, the human race, is the most difficult of all material to handle. It is almost as dangerous as an explosive.

No doubt it is true that in the machinery of the State the freedom of the press performs the same function as a safety-valve in other machinery; for it enables all discontent to find a voice; nay, in doing so, the discontent exhausts itself if it has not much substance; and if it has, there is an advantage in recognising it betimes and applying the remedy. This is much better than to repress the discontent, and let it simmer and ferment, and go on increasing until it ends in an explosion. On the other hand, the freedom of the press may be regarded as a permission to sell poison—poison for the heart and the mind. There is no idea so foolish but that it cannot be put into the heads of the ignorant and incapable multitude, especially if the idea holds out some prospect of any gain or advantage. And when a man has got hold of any such idea what is there that he will not do? I am, therefore, very much afraid that the danger of a free press outweighs its utility, particularly where the law offers a way of redressing wrongs. In any case, however, the freedom of the press should be governed by a very strict prohibition of all and every anonymity.

Generally, indeed, it may be maintained that right is of a nature analogous to that of certain chemical substances, which cannot be exhibited in a pure and isolated condition, but at the most only with a small admixture of some other substance, which serves as a vehicle for them, or gives them the necessary consistency; such as fluorine, or even alcohol, or prussic acid. Pursuing the analogy we may say that right, if it is to gain a footing in the world and really prevail, must of necessity be supplemented by a small amount of arbitrary force, in order that, notwithstanding its merely ideal and therefore ethereal nature, it may be able to work and subsist in the real and material world, and not evaporate and vanish into the clouds, as it does in Hesiod. Birthright of every description, all heritable privileges, every form of national religion, and so on, may be regarded as the necessary chemical base or alloy; inasmuch as it is only when right has some such firm and actual foundation that it can be enforced and consistently vindicated. They form for right a sort of ός μοί ποῦ στῶ—a fulcrum for supporting its lever.

Linnæus adopted a vegetable system of an artificial and arbitrary character. It cannot be replaced by a natural one, no matter how reasonable the change might be, or how often it has been attempted to make it, because no other system could ever yield the same certainty and stability of definition. Just in the same way the artificial and arbitrary basis on which, as has been shown, the constitution of a State rests, can never be replaced by a purely natural basis. A natural basis would aim at doing away with the conditions that have been mentioned: in the place of the privileges of birth it would put those of personal merit; in the place of the national religion, the results of rationalistic inquiry, and so on. However agreeable to reason this might all prove, the change could not be made; because a natural basis would lack that certainty and fixity of definition which alone secures the stability of the commonwealth. A constitution which embodied abstract right alone would be an excellent thing for natures other than human, but since the great majority of men are extremely egoistic, unjust, inconsiderate, deceitful, and sometimes even malicious; since in addition they are endowed with very scanty intelligence there arises the necessity for a power that shall be concentrated in one man, a power that shall be above all law and right, and be completely irresponsible, nay, to which everything shall yield as to something that is regarded as a creature of a higher kind, a ruler by the grace of God. It is only thus that men can be permanently held in check and governed.

The United States of North America exhibit the attempt to proceed without any such arbitrary basis; that is to say, to allow abstract right to prevail pure and unalloyed. But the result is not attractive. For with all the material prosperity of the country what do we find? The prevailing sentiment is a base Utilitarianism with its inevitable companion, ignorance; and it is this that has paved the way for a union of stupid Anglican bigotry, foolish prejudice, coarse brutality, and a childish veneration of women. Even worse things are the order of the day: most iniquitous oppression of the black freedmen, lynch law, frequent assassination often committed with entire impunity, duels of a savagery elsewhere unknown, now and then open scorn of all law and justice, repudiation of public debts, abominable political rascality towards a neighbouring State, followed by a mercenary raid on its rich territory,—afterwards sought to be excused, on the part of the chief authority of the State, by lies which every one in the country knew to be such and laughed at—an ever-increasing ochlocracy, and finally all the disastrous influence which this abnegation of justice in high quarters must have exercised on private morals. This specimen of a pure constitution on the obverse side of the planet says very little for republics in general, but still less for the imitations of it in Mexico, Guatemala, Colombia and Peru.

A peculiar disadvantage attaching to republics—and one that might not be looked for—is that in this form of government it must be more difficult for men of ability to attain high position and exercise direct political influence than in the case of monarchies. For always and everywhere and under all circumstances there is a conspiracy, or instinctive alliance, against such men on the part of all the stupid, the weak, and the commonplace; they look upon such men as their natural enemies, and they are firmly held together by a common fear of them. There is always a numer-

ous host of the stupid and the weak, and in a republican constitution it is easy for them to suppress and exclude the men of ability,
so that they may not be outflanked by them. They are fifty to one;
and here all have equal rights at the start.

In a monarchy, on the other hand, this natural and universal
league of the stupid against those who are possessed of intellectual
advantages is a one-sided affair; it exists only from below, for in a
monarchy talent and intelligence receive a natural advocacy and
support from above. In the first place, the position of the monarch
himself is much too high and too firm for him to stand in fear
of any sort of competition. In the next place, he serves the State
more by his will than by his intelligence; for no intelligence could
ever be equal to all the demands that would in his case be made
upon it. He is therefore compelled to be always availing himself of
other men's intelligence. Seeing that his own interests are securely
bound up with those of his country; that they are inseparable from
them and one with them, he will naturally give the preference to
the best men, because they are his most serviceable instruments,
and he will bestow his favour upon them—as soon, that is, as he
can find them; which is not so difficult, if only an honest search be
made. Just in the same way even ministers of State have too much
advantage over rising politicians to need to regard them with jeal-
ousy; and accordingly for analogous reasons they are glad to single
out distinguished men and set them to work, in order to make use
of their powers for themselves. It is in this way that intelligence
has always under a monarchical government a much better chance
against its irreconcilable and ever-present foe, stupidity; and the
advantage which it gains is very great.

In general, the monarchical form of government is that which
is natural to man; just as it is natural to bees and ants, to a flight
of cranes, a herd of wandering elephants, a pack of wolves seeking
prey in common, and many other animals, all of which place one
of their number at the head of the business in hand. Every business
in which men engage, if it is attended with danger—every cam-
paign, every ship at sea—must also be subject to the authority of
one commander; everywhere it is one will that must lead. Even the
animal organism is constructed on a monarchical principle: it is the

brain alone which guides and governs, and exercises the hegemony. Although heart, lungs, and stomach contribute much more to the continued existence of the whole body, these philistines cannot on that account be allowed to guide and lead. That is a business which belongs solely to the brain; government must proceed from one central point. Even the solar system is monarchical. On the other hand, a republic is as unnatural as it is unfavourable to the higher intellectual life and the arts and sciences. Accordingly we find that everywhere in the world, and at all times, nations, whether civilised or savage, or occupying a position between the two, are always under monarchical government. The rule of many as Homer said, is not a good thing: let there be one ruler, one king:—

> Οὐκ ἀγαθόν πολυκοιράνιη · εἷς κοίρανος ἔστω
> Εἷς βασιλεύς.[1]

How would it be possible that, everywhere and at all times, we should see many millions of people, nay, even hundreds of millions, become the willing and obedient subjects of one man, sometimes even one woman, and provisionally, even, of a child, unless there were a monarchical instinct in men which drove them to it as the form of government best suited to them? This arrangement is not the product of reflection. Everywhere one man is king, and for the most part his dignity is hereditary. He is, as it were, the personification, the monogram, of the whole people, which attains an individuality in him. In this sense he can rightly say: *l'etat c'est moi.* It is precisely for this reason that in Shakespeare's historical plays the kings of England and France mutually address each other as *France* and *England,* and the Duke of Austria goes by the name of his country. It is as though the kings regarded themselves as the incarnation of their nationalities. It is all in accordance with human nature; and for this very reason the hereditary monarch cannot separate his own welfare and that of his family from the welfare of his country; as, on the other hand, mostly happens when the monarch is elected, as, for instance, in the States of the Church.[2]

---

[1] *Iliad,* ii., 204.
[2] *Translator's Note.* The reader will recollect that Schopenhauer was writing long before the Papal territories were absorbed into the kingdom of Italy.

The Chinese can conceive of a monarchical government only; what a republic is they utterly fail to understand. When a Dutch legation was in China in the year 1658, it was obliged to represent that the Prince of Orange was their king, as otherwise the Chinese would have been inclined to take Holland for a nest of pirates living without any lord or master.[1] Stobæus, in a chapter in his *Florilegium,* at the head of which he wrote *That monarchy is best,* collected the best of the passages in which the ancients explained the advantages of that form of government. In a word, republics are unnatural and artificial; they are the product of reflection. Hence it is that they occur only as rare exceptions in the whole history of the world. There were the small Greek republics, the Roman and the Carthaginian; but they were all rendered possible by the fact that five-sixths, perhaps even seven-eighths, of the population consisted of slaves. In the year 1840, even in the United States, there were three million slaves to a population of sixteen millions. Then, again, the duration of the republics of antiquity, compared with that of monarchies, was very short. Republics are very easy to found, and very difficult to maintain, while with monarchies it is exactly the reverse. If it is Utopian schemes that are wanted, I say this: the only solution of the problem would be a despotism of the wise and the noble, of the true aristocracy and the genuine nobility, brought about by the method of generation—that is, by the marriage of the noblest men with the cleverest and most intellectual women. This is my Utopia, my Republic of Plato.

Constitutional kings are undoubtedly in much the same position as the gods of Epicurus, who sit up on high in undisturbed bliss and tranquillity, and do not meddle with human affairs. Just now they are the fashion. In every German duodecimo-principality a parody of the English constitution is set up, quite complete, from Upper and Lower Houses down to the Habeas Corpus Act and trial by jury. These institutions, which proceed from English character and English circumstances, and presuppose both, are natural and suitable to the English people. It is just as natural to the German people to

---

[1] See Jean Nieuhoff, *L'Ambassade de la Compagnie Orientale des Provinces Unies vers L'Empereur de la Chine,* traduit par Jean le Charpentier à Leyde, 1665, ch. 45.

be split up into a number of different stocks, under a similar number of ruling Princes, with an Emperor over them all, who maintains peace at home, and represents the unity of the State abroad. It is an arrangement which has proceeded from German character and German circumstances. I am of opinion that if Germany is not to meet with the same fate as Italy, it must restore the imperial crown, which was done away with by its arch-enemy, the first Napoleon; and it must restore it as effectively as possible.[1] For German unity depends on it, and without the imperial crown it will always be merely nominal, or precarious. But as we no longer live in the days of Günther of Schwarzburg, when the choice of Emperor was a serious business, the imperial crown ought to go alternately to Prussia and to Austria, for the life of the wearer. In any case, the absolute sovereignty of the small States is illusory. Napoleon I. did for Germany what Otto the Great did for Italy: he divided it into small, independent States, on the principle, *divide et impera.*

The English show their great intelligence, amongst other ways, by clinging to their ancient institutions, customs and usages, and by holding them sacred, even at the risk of carrying this tenacity too far, and making it ridiculous. They hold them sacred for the simple reason that those institutions and customs are not the invention of an idle head, but have grown up gradually by the force of circumstance and the wisdom of life itself, and are therefore suited to them as a nation. On the other hand, the German Michel[2] allows himself to be persuaded by his schoolmaster that he must go about in an English dress-coat, and that nothing else will do. Accordingly he has bullied his father into giving it to him;

---

[1] *Translator's Note.* Here, again, it is hardly necessary to say that Schopenhauer, who died in 1860, and wrote this passage at least some years previously, cannot be referring to any of the events which culminated in 1870. The whole passage forms a striking illustration of his political sagacity.

[2] *Translator's Note.* It may be well to explain that "Michel" is sometimes used by the Germans as a nickname of their nation, corresponding to "John Bull" as a nickname of the English. Flügel in his German-English Dictionary declares that *der deutsche Michel* represents the German nation as an honest, blunt, unsuspicious fellow, who easily allows himself to be imposed upon, even, he adds, with a touch of patriotism, "by those who are greatly his inferiors in point of strength and real worth."

and with his awkward manners this ungainly creature presents in
it a sufficiently ridiculous figure. But the dress-coat will some day
be too tight for him and incommode him. It will not be very
long before he feels it in trial by jury. This institution arose in the
most barbarous period of the Middle Ages—the times of Alfred
the Great, when the ability to read and write exempted a man
from the penalty of death. It is the worst of all criminal proce-
dures. Instead of judges, well versed in law and of great experience,
who have grown grey in daily unravelling the tricks and wiles of
thieves, murderers and rascals of all sorts, and so are well able to get
at the bottom of things, it is gossiping tailors and tanners who sit in
judgment; it is their coarse, crude, unpractised, and awkward intelligence, incapable of any sustained attention, that is called upon
to find out the truth from a tissue of lies and deceit. All the time,
moreover, they are thinking of their cloth and their leather, and
longing to be at home; and they have absolutely no clear notion at
all of the distinction between probability and certainty. It is with
this sort of a calculus of probabilities in their stupid heads that they
confidently undertake to seal a man's doom.

The same remark is applicable to them which Dr. Johnson made
of a court-martial in which he had little confidence, summoned
to decide a very important case. He said that perhaps there was
not a member of it who, in the whole course of his life, had ever
spent an hour by himself in balancing probabilities.[1] Can any one
imagine that the tailor and the tanner would be impartial judges?
What! the vicious multitude impartial! as if partiality were not ten
times more to be feared from men of the same class as the accused
than from judges who knew nothing of him personally, lived in
another sphere altogether, were irremovable, and conscious of the
dignity of their office. But to let a jury decide on crimes against
the State and its head, or on misdemeanours of the press, is in a
very real sense to set the fox to keep the geese.

Everywhere and at all times there has been much discontent
with governments, laws and public regulations; for the most
part, however, because men are always ready to make institutions

---

[1] Boswell's *Johnson,* 1780, æt.71.

responsible for the misery inseparable from human existence itself; which is, to speak mythically, the curse that was laid on Adam, and through him on the whole race. But never has that delusion been proclaimed in a more mendacious and impudent manner than by the demagogues of the *Jetztzeit*—of the day we live in. As enemies of Christianity, they are, of course, optimists: to them the world is its own end and object, and accordingly in itself, that is to say, in its own natural constitution, it is arranged on the most excellent principles, and forms a regular habitation of bliss. The enormous and glaring evils of the world they attribute wholly to governments: if governments, they think, were to do their duty, there would be a heaven upon earth; in other words, all men could eat, drink, propagate and die, free from trouble and want. This is what they mean when they talk of the world being "its own end and object"; this is the goal of that "perpetual progress of the human race," and the other fine things which they are never tired of proclaiming.

Formerly it was *faith* which was the chief support of the throne; nowadays it is *credit*. The Pope himself is scarcely more concerned to retain the confidence of the faithful than to make his creditors believe in his own good faith. If in times past it was the guilty debt of the world which was lamented, now it is the financial debts of the world which arouse dismay. Formerly it was the Last Day which was prophesied; now it is the σεισάχθεια the great repudiation, the universal bankruptcy of the nations, which will one day happen; although the prophet, in this as in the other case, entertains a firm hope that he will not live to see it himself.

★ ★ ★ ★ ★

From an ethical and a rational point of view, the *right of possession* rests upon an incomparably better foundation than the *right of birth;* nevertheless, the right of possession is allied with the right of birth and has come to be part and parcel of it, so that it would hardly be possible to abolish the right of birth without endangering the right of possession. The reason of this is that most of what a man possesses he inherited, and therefore holds by a kind of right of birth; just as the old nobility bear the names only of their hereditary estates, and by the use of those names do no more than give expression to the fact that they own the estates. Accordingly all owners of property, if instead of being envious they were wise, ought also to support the maintenance of the rights of birth.

The existence of a nobility has, then, a double advantage: it helps to maintain on the one hand the rights of possession, and on the other the right of birth belonging to the king. For the king is the first nobleman in the country, and, as a general rule, he treats the nobility as his humble relations, and regards them quite otherwise than the commoners, however trusty and well-beloved. It is quite natural, too, that he should have more confidence in those whose ancestors were mostly the first ministers, and always the immediate associates, of his own. A nobleman, therefore, appeals with reason to the name he bears, when, on the occurrence of anything to rouse distrust he repeats his assurance of fidelity and service to the king. A man's character, as my readers are aware, assuredly comes to him from his father. It is a narrow-minded and ridiculous thing not to consider whose son a man is.

Free-will and Fatalism

No thoughtful man can have any doubt, after the conclusions reached in my prize-essay on *Moral Freedom,* that such freedom is to be sought, not anywhere in nature, but outside of it. The only freedom that exists is of a metaphysical character. In the physical world freedom is an impossibility. Accordingly, while our several actions are in no wise free, every man's individual character is to be regarded as a free act. He is such and such a man, because once for all it is his will to be that man. For the will itself, and in itself, and also in so far as it is manifest in an individual, and accordingly constitutes the original and fundamental desires of that individual, is independent of all knowledge, because it is antecedent to such knowledge. All that it receives from knowledge is the series of motives by which it successively develops its nature and makes itself cognisable or visible; but the will itself, as something that lies beyond time, and so long as it exists at all, never changes. Therefore every man, being what he is and placed in the circumstances which for the moment obtain, but which on their part also arise by strict necessity, can absolutely never do anything else than just what at that moment he does do. Accordingly, the whole course of a man's life, in all its incidents great and small, is as necessarily predetermined as the course of a clock.

The main reason of this is that the kind of metaphysical free act which I have described tends to become a knowing consciousness—a perceptive intuition, which is subject to the forms of space and time. By means of those forms the unity and indivisibility of the act are represented as drawn asunder into a series of states and events, which are subject to the Principle of Sufficient Reason in its four forms— and it is this that is meant by *necessity.* But the result of it all assumes a moral complexion. It amounts to this, that by what we do we know what we are, and by what we suffer we know what we deserve.

Further, it follows from this that a man's *individuality* does not rest upon the principle of individuation alone, and therefore is not altogether phenomenal in its nature. On the contrary, it has its roots in the thing-in-itself, in the will which is the essence of each individual. The character of this individual is itself individual. But how deep the roots of individuality extend is one of the questions which I do not undertake to answer.

In this connection it deserves to be mentioned that even Plato, in his own way, represented the individuality of a man as a free act.[1] He represented him as coming into the world with a given tendency, which was the result of the feelings and character already attaching to him in accordance with the doctrine of metempsychosis. The Brahmin philosophers also express the unalterable fixity of innate character in a mystical fashion. They say that Brahma, when a man is produced, engraves his doings and sufferings in written characters on his skull, and that his life must take shape in accordance therewith. They point to the jagged edges in the sutures of the skull-bones as evidence of this writing; and the purport of it, they say, depends on his previous life and actions. The same view appears to underlie the Christian, or rather, the Pauline, dogma of Predestination.

But this truth, which is universally confirmed by experience, is attended with another result. All genuine merit, moral as well as intellectual, is not merely physical or empirical in its origin, but metaphysical; that is to say, it is given *à priori* and not *à posteriori;* in other words, it lies innate and is not acquired, and therefore its source is not a mere phenomenon, but the thing-in-itself. Hence it is that every man achieves only that which is irrevocably established in his nature, or is born with him. Intellectual capacity needs, it is true, to be developed just as many natural products need to be cultivated in order that we may enjoy or use them; but just as in the case of a natural product no cultivation can take the place of original material, neither can it do so in the case of intellect. That is the reason why qualities which are merely acquired, or learned, or enforced—that is, qualities *à posteriori,* whether moral

---

[1] *Phædrus* and *Laws, bk.* x.

or intellectual—are not real or genuine, but superficial only, and possessed of no value. This is a conclusion of true metaphysics, and experience teaches the same lesson to all who can look below the surface. Nay, it is proved by the great importance which we all attach to such innate characteristics as physiognomy and external appearance, in the case of a man who is at all distinguished; and that is why we are so curious to see him. Superficial people, to be sure,—and, for very good reasons, commonplace people too,—will be of the opposite opinion; for if anything fails them they will thus be enabled to console themselves by thinking that it is still to come.

The world, then, is not merely a battlefield where victory and defeat receive their due recompense in a future state. No! the world is itself the Last Judgment on it. Every man carries with him the reward and the disgrace that he deserves; and this is no other than the doctrine of the Brahmins and Buddhists as it is taught in the theory of metempsychosis.

The question has been raised, What two men would do, who lived a solitary life in the wilds and met each other for the first time. Hobbes, Pufendorf, and Rousseau have given different answers. Pufendorf believed that they would approach each other as friends; Hobbes, on the contrary, as enemies; Rousseau, that they would pass each other by in silence. All three are both right and wrong. This is just a case in which the incalculable difference that there is in innate moral disposition between one individual and another would make its appearance. The difference is so strong that the question here raised might be regarded as the standard and measure of it. For there are men in whom the sight of another man at once rouses a feeling of enmity, since their inmost nature exclaims at once: That is not me! There are, others in whom the sight awakens immediate sympathy; their inmost nature says: *That is me over again!* Between the two there are countless degrees. That in this most important matter we are so totally different is a great problem, nay, a mystery.

In regard to this *à priori* nature of moral character there is matter for varied reflection in a work by Bastholm, a Danish writer, entitled *Historical Contributions to the Knowledge of Man in the Savage*

State. He is struck by the fact that intellectual culture and moral excellence are shown to be entirely independent of each other, inasmuch as one is often found without the other. The reason of this, as we shall find, is simply that moral excellence in no wise springs from reflection, which is developed by intellectual culture, but from the will itself, the constitution of which is innate and not susceptible in itself of any improvement by means of education. Bastholm represents most nations as very vicious and immoral; and on the other hand he reports that excellent traits of character are found amongst some savage peoples; as, for instance, amongst the Orotchyses, the inhabitants of the island Savu, the Tunguses, and the Pelew islanders. He thus attempts to solve the problem, How it is that some tribes are so remarkably good, when their neighbours are all bad.

It seems to me that the difficulty may be explained as follows: Moral qualities, as we know, are heritable, and an isolated tribe, such as is described, might take its rise in some one family, and ultimately in a single ancestor who happened to be a good man, and then maintain its purity. Is it not the case, for instance, that on many unpleasant occasions, such as repudiation of public debts, filibustering raids and so on, the English have often reminded the North Americans of their descent from English penal colonists? It is a reproach, however, which can apply only to a small part of the population.

It is marvellous how *every man's individuality* (that is to say, the union of a definite character with a definite intellect) accurately determines all his actions and thoughts down to the most unimportant details, as though it were a dye which pervaded them; and how, in consequence, one man's whole course of life, in other words, his inner and outer history, turns out so absolutely different from another's. As a botanist knows a plant in its entirety from a single leaf; as Cuvier from a single bone constructed the whole animal, so an accurate knowledge of a man's whole character may be attained from a single characteristic act; that is to say, he himself may to some extent be constructed from it, even though the act in question is of very trifling consequence. Nay, that is the most perfect test of all, for in a matter of importance people are on their guard; in trifles they follow their natural bent without much reflection. That is why Seneca's remark, that even the smallest things may be taken as evidence of character, is so true: *argumenta morum ex minimis quoque licet capere.*[1] If a man shows by his absolutely unscrupulous and selfish behaviour in small things that a sentiment of justice is foreign to his disposition, he should not be trusted with a penny unless on due security. For who will believe that the man who every day shows that he is unjust in all matters other than those which concern property, and whose boundless selfishness everywhere protrudes through the small affairs of ordinary life which are subject to no scrutiny, like a dirty shirt through the holes of a ragged jacket—who, I ask, will believe that such a man will act honourably in matters of *meum* and *tuum* without any other incentive but that of justice? The man who has no conscience in small things will be a scoundrel in big things. If we neglect small traits of character, we have only ourselves to blame if we afterwards learn to our disadvantage what this character is in the great affairs of life. On the same principle, we ought to break with so-called friends even in matters of trifling moment, if they show a character that is malicious or bad or vulgar, so that we may avoid the bad turn which only waits for an opportunity of being done us. The same thing applies to servants. Let it always be our maxim: Better alone than amongst traitors.

Of a truth the first and foremost step in all knowledge of mankind is the conviction that a man's conduct, taken as a whole, and in all its essential particulars, is not governed by his reason or by any of the resolutions which he may make in virtue of it. No man becomes this or that by wishing to be it, however earnestly. His acts proceed from his innate and unalterable character, and they are more immediately and particularly determined by motives. A man's conduct, therefore, is the necessary product of both character and motive. It may be illustrated by the course of a planet, which is the result of the combined effect of the tangential energy with which it is endowed, and the centripetal energy which operates from the sun. In this simile the former energy represents character, and the

---

[1] *Ep.*, 52.

latter the influence of motive. It is almost more than a mere simile. The tangential energy which properly speaking is the source of the planet's motion, whilst on the other hand the motion is kept in check by gravitation, is, from a metaphysical point of view, the will manifesting itself in that body.

To grasp this fact is to see that we really never form anything more than a conjecture of what we shall do under circumstances which are still to happen; although we often take our conjecture for a resolve. When, for instance, in pursuance of a proposal, a man with the greatest sincerity, and even eagerness, accepts an engagement to do this or that on the occurrence of a certain future event, it is by no means certain that he will fulfil the engagement; unless he is so constituted that the promise which he gives, in itself and as such, is always and everywhere a motive sufficient for him, by acting upon him, through considerations of honour, like some external compulsion. But above and beyond this, what he will do on the occurrence of that event may be foretold from true and accurate knowledge of his character and the external circumstances under the influence of which he will fall; and it may with complete certainty be foretold from this alone. Nay, it is a very easy prophecy if he has been already seen in a like position; for he will inevitably do the same thing a second time, provided that on the first occasion he had a true and complete knowledge of the facts of the case. For, as I have often remarked, a final cause does not impel a man by being real, but by being known; *causa finalis non movet secundum suum esse reale, sed secundum esse cognitum.*[1] Whatever he failed to recognise or understand the first time could have no influence upon his will; just as an electric current stops when some isolating body hinders the action of the conductor. This unalterable nature of character, and the consequent necessity of our actions, are made very clear to a man who has not, on any given occasion, behaved as he ought to have done, by showing a lack either of resolution or endurance or courage, or some other quality demanded at the moment. Afterwards he recognises what it is that he ought to have done; and, sincerely repenting of his incorrect behaviour, he thinks to

---

[1] Suarez, *Disp. Metaph.*, xxiii.; §§7 and 8.

himself, *If the opportunity were offered to me again, I should act differently.* It is offered once more; the same occasion recurs; and to his great astonishment he does precisely the same thing over again.[1]

The best examples of the truth in question are in every way furnished by Shakespeare's plays. It is a truth with which he was thoroughly imbued, and his intuitive wisdom expressed it in a concrete shape on every page. I shall here, however, give an instance of it in a case in which he makes it remarkably clear, without exhibiting any design or affectation in the matter; for he was a real artist and never set out from general ideas. His method was obviously to work up to the psychological truth which he grasped directly and intuitively, regardless of the fact that few would notice or understand it, and without the smallest idea that some dull and shallow fellows in Germany would one day proclaim far and wide that he wrote his works to illustrate moral commonplaces. I allude to the character of the Earl of Northumberland, whom we find in three plays in succession, although he does not take a leading part in any one of them; nay, he appears only in a few scenes distributed over fifteen acts. Consequently, if the reader is not very attentive, a character exhibited at such great intervals, and its moral identity, may easily escape his notice, even though it has by no means escaped the poet's. He makes the earl appear everywhere with a noble and knightly grace, and talk in language suitable to it; nay, he sometimes puts very beautiful and even elevated passages, into his mouth. At the same time he is very far from writing after the manner of Schiller, who was fond of painting the devil black, and whose moral approval or disapproval of the characters which he represented could be heard in their own words. With Shakespeare, and also with Goethe, every character, as long as he is on the stage and speaking, seems to be absolutely in the right, even though it were the devil himself. In this respect let the reader compare Duke Alba as he appears in Goethe with the same character in Schiller.

We make the acquaintance of the Earl of Northumberland in the play of *Richard II.,* where he is the first to hatch a plot against the King in favour of Bolingbroke, afterwards Henry IV., to whom he

---

[1]Cf. *World as Will,* ii., pp. 251 ff. *sqq.* (third edition).

even offers some personal flattery (Act II., Sc. 3). In the following act he suffers a reprimand because, in speaking of the King he talks of him as "Richard," without more ado, but protests that he did it only for brevity's sake. A little later his insidious words induce the King to surrender. In the following act, when the King renounces the crown, Northumberland treats him with such harshness and contempt that the unlucky monarch is quite broken, and losing all patience once more exclaims to him: *Fiend, thou torment'st me ere I come to hell!* At the close, Northumberland announces to the new King that he has sent the heads of the former King's adherents to London.

In the following tragedy, *Henry IV.,* he hatches a plot against the new King in just the same way. In the fourth act we see the rebels united, making preparations for the decisive battle on the morrow, and only waiting impatiently for Northumberland and his division. At last there arrives a letter from him, saying that he is ill, and that he cannot entrust his force to any one else; but that nevertheless the others should go forward with courage and make a brave fight. They do so, but, greatly weakened by his absence, they are completely defeated; most of their leaders are captured, and his own son, the valorous Hotspur, falls by the hand of the Prince of Wales.

Again, in the following play, the *Second Part of Henry IV.,* we see him reduced to a state of the fiercest wrath by the death of his son, and maddened by the thirst for revenge. Accordingly he kindles another rebellion, and the heads of it assemble once more. In the fourth act, just as they are about to give battle, and are only waiting for him to join them, there comes a letter saying that he cannot collect a proper force, and will therefore seek safety for the present in Scotland; that, nevertheless, he heartily wishes their heroic undertaking the best success. Thereupon they surrender to the King under a treaty which is not kept, and so perish.

So far is character from being the work of reasoned choice and consideration that in any action the intellect has nothing to do but to present motives to the will. Thereafter it looks on as a mere spectator and witness at the course which life takes, in accordance with the influence of motive on the given character. All the incidents of life occur, strictly speaking, with the same necessity as the movement of a clock. On this point let me refer to my prize-essay on *The Freedom of the Will*. I have there explained the true meaning and origin of the persistent illusion that the will is entirely free in every single action; and I have indicated the cause to which it is due. I will only add here the following teleological explanation of this natural illusion.

Since every single action of a man's life seems to possess the freedom and originality which in truth only belong to his character as he apprehends it, and the mere apprehension of it by his intellect is what constitutes his career; and since what is original in every single action seems to the empirical consciousness to be always being performed anew, a man thus receives in the course of his career the strongest possible moral lesson. Then, and not before, he becomes thoroughly conscious of all the bad sides of his character. Conscience accompanies every act with the comment: *You could act differently,* although its true sense is: *You could be other than you are.* As the result of this immutability of character on the one hand, and, on the other, of the strict necessity which attends all the circumstances in which character is successively placed, every man's course of life is precisely determined from Alpha right through to Omega. But, nevertheless, one man's course of life turns out immeasurably happier, nobler and more worthy than another's, whether it be regarded from a subjective or an objective point of view, and unless we are to exclude all ideas of justice, we are led to the doctrine which is well accepted in Brahminism and Buddhism, that the subjective conditions in which, as well as the objective conditions under which, every man is born, are the moral consequences of a previous existence.

Macchiavelli, who seems to have taken no interest whatever in philosophical speculations, is drawn by the keen subtlety of his very unique understanding into the following observation, which possesses a really deep meaning. It shows that he had an intuitive knowledge of the entire necessity with which, characters and motives being given, all actions take place. He makes it at the beginning of the prologue to his comedy *Clitia. If,* he says, *the same men were to recur in the world in the way that the same circumstances recur, a hundred years would never elapse without our finding ourselves together once more, and doing the same things as we are doing now—Se nel mondo tornassino i medesimi uomini, como tornano i medesimi casi, non passarebbono mai cento anni che noi non ci trovassimo un altra volta insieme, a fare le medesime cose che hora.* He seems however to have been drawn into the remark by a reminiscence of what Augustine says in his *De Civitate Dei,* bk. xii., ch. xiii.

Again, Fate, or the εἱμαρμένη of the ancients, is nothing but the conscious certainty that all that happens is fast bound by a chain of causes, and therefore takes place with a strict necessity; that the future is already ordained with absolute certainty and can undergo as little alteration as the past. In the fatalistic myths of the ancients all that can be regarded as fabulous is the prediction of the future; that is, if we refuse to consider the possibility of magnetic clairvoyance and second sight. Instead of trying to explain away the fundamental truth of Fatalism by superficial twaddle and foolish evasion, a man should attempt to get a clear knowledge and comprehension of it; for it is demonstrably true, and it helps us in a very important way to an understanding of the mysterious riddle of our life. Predestination and Fatalism do not differ in the main. They differ only in this, that with Predestination the given character and external determination of human action proceed from a rational Being, and with Fatalism from an irrational one. But in either case the result is the same: that happens which must happen.

On the other hand the conception of *Moral Freedom* is inseparable from that of *Originality.* A man may be said, but he cannot be conceived, to be the work of another, and at the same time be free in respect of his desires and acts. He who called him into existence out of nothing in the same process created and determined his nature—in other words, the whole of his qualities. For no one can create without creating a something, that is to say, a being determined throughout and in all its qualities. But all that a man says and does necessarily proceeds from the qualities so determined; for it is only the qualities themselves set in motion. It is only some external impulse that they require to make their appearance. As a man is, so must he act; and praise or blame attaches, not to his separate acts, but to his nature and being.

That is the reason why Theism and the moral responsibility of man are incompatible; because responsibility always reverts to the

creator of man and it is there that it has its centre. Vain attempts
have been made to make a bridge from one of these incompatibles
to the other by means of the conception of moral freedom; but
it always breaks down again. What is *free* must also be *original*. If
our will is *free,* our will is also *the original element,* and conversely.
Pre-Kantian dogmatism tried to separate these two predicaments.
It was thereby compelled to assume two kinds of freedom, one
cosmological, of the first cause, and the other moral and theological, of human will. These are represented in Kant by the third as
well as the fourth antinomy of freedom.

On the other hand, in my philosophy the plain recognition of
the strictly necessary character of all action is in accordance with
the doctrine that what manifests itself even in the inorganic and
irrational world is *will*. If this were not so, the necessity under
which irrational beings obviously act would place their action in
conflict with will; if, I mean, there were really such a thing as the
freedom of individual action, and this were not as strictly neces-
sitated as every other kind of action. But, as I have just shown,
it is this same doctrine of the necessary character of all acts of
will which makes it needful to regard a man's existence and being
as itself the work of his freedom, and consequently of his will.
The will, therefore, must be self-existent; it must possess so-called
a-se-ity. Under the opposite supposition all responsibility, as I have
shown, would be at an end, and the moral like the physical world
would be a mere machine, set in motion for the amusement of its
manufacturer placed somewhere outside of it. So it is that truths
hang together, and mutually advance and complete one another;
whereas error gets jostled at every corner.

★ ★ ★ ★ ★

What kind of influence it is that *moral instruction* may exercise
on conduct, and what are the limits of that influence, are questions
which I have sufficiently examined in the twentieth section of my
treatise on the *Foundation of Morality*. In all essential particulars an
analogous influence is exercised by *example,* which, however, has
a more powerful effect than doctrine, and therefore it deserves a
brief analysis.

In the main, example works either by restraining a man or by encouraging him. It has the former effect when it determines him to leave undone what he wanted to do. He sees, I mean, that other people do not do it; and from this he judges, in general, that it is not expedient; that it may endanger his person, or his property, or his honour. He rests content, and gladly finds himself relieved from examining into the matter for himself. Or he may see that another man, who has not refrained, has incurred evil consequences from doing it; this is example of the deterrent kind. The example which encourages a man works in a twofold manner. It either induces him to do what he would be glad to leave undone, if he were not afraid lest the omission might in some way endanger him, or injure him in others' opinion; or else it encourages him to do what he is glad to do, but has hitherto refrained from doing from fear of danger or shame; this is example of the seductive kind. Finally, example may bring a man to do what he would have otherwise never thought of doing. It is obvious that in this last case example works in the main only on the intellect; its effect on the will is secondary, and if it has any such effect, it is by the interposition of the man's own judgment, or by reliance on the person who presented the example.

The whole influence of example—and it is very strong—rests on the fact that a man has, as a rule, too little judgment of his own, and often too little knowledge, to explore his own way for himself, and that he is glad, therefore, to tread in the footsteps of some one else. Accordingly, the more deficient he is in either of these qualities, the more is he open to the influence of example; and we find, in fact, that most men's guiding star is the example of others; that their whole course of life, in great things and in small, comes in the end to be mere imitation; and that not even in the pettiest matters do they act according to their own judgment. Imitation and custom are the spring of almost all human action. The cause of it is that men fight shy of all and any sort of reflection, and very properly mistrust their own discernment. At the same time this remarkably strong imitative instinct in man is a proof of his kinship with apes.

But the kind of effect which example exercises depends upon a man's character, and thus it is that the same example may possibly seduce one man and deter another. An easy opportunity of observing this is afforded in the case of certain social impertinences which come into vogue and gradually spread. The first time that a man notices anything of the kind, he may say to himself: *For shame! how can he do it! how selfish and inconsiderate of him! really, I shall take care never to do anything like that.* But twenty others will think: *Aha! if he does that, I may do it too.*

As regards morality, example, like doctrine, may, it is true, promote civil or legal amelioration, but not that inward amendment which is, strictly speaking, the only kind of moral amelioration. For example always works as a personal motive alone, and assumes, therefore, that a man is susceptible to this sort of motive. But it is just the predominating sensitiveness of a character to this or that sort of motive that determines whether its morality is true and real; though, of whatever kind it is, it is always innate. In general it may be said that example operates as a means of promoting the good and the bad qualities of a character, but it does not create them; and so it is that Seneca's maxim, *velle non discitur—will cannot be learned—*also holds good here. But the innateness of all truly moral qualities, of the good as of the bad, is a doctrine that consorts better with the metempsychosis of the Brahmins and Buddhists, according to which a man's good and bad deeds follow him from one existence to another like his shadow, than with Judaism. For Judaism requires a man to come into the world as a moral blank, so that, in virtue of an inconceivable free will, directed to objects which are neither to be sought nor avoided—*liberum arbitrium indifferentiæ—*and consequently as the result of reasoned consideration, he may choose whether he is to be an angel or a devil, or anything else that may lie between the two. Though I am well aware what the Jewish scheme is, I pay no attention to it; for my standard is truth. I am no professor of philosophy, and therefore I do not find my vocation in establishing the fundamental ideas of Judaism at any cost, even though they for ever bar the way to all and every kind of philosophical knowledge. *Liberum arbitrium indifferentiæ* under the name of *moral freedom* is a charming doll for professors of philosophy to dandle; and we must leave it to those intelligent, honourable and upright gentlemen.

Character

Men who aspire to a happy, a brilliant and a long life, instead of to a virtuous one, are like foolish actors who want to be always having the great parts,—the parts that are marked by splendour and triumph. They fail to see that the important thing is not *what* or *how much,* but *how* they act.

Since *a man does not alter,* and his *moral character* remains absolutely the same all through his life; since he must play out the part which he has received, without the least deviation from the character; since neither experience, nor philosophy, nor religion can effect any improvement in him, the question arises, What is the meaning of life at all? To what purpose is it played, this farce in which everything that is essential is irrevocably fixed and determined?

It is played that a man may come to understand himself, that he may see what it is that he seeks and has sought to be; what he wants, and what, therefore, he is. *This is a knowledge which must be imparted to him from without.* Life is to man, in other words, to will, what chemical re-agents are to the body: it is only by life that a man reveals what he is, and it is only in so far as he reveals himself that he exists at all. Life is the manifestation of character, of the something that we understand by that word; and it is not in life, but outside of it, and outside time, that character undergoes alteration, as a result of the self-knowledge which life gives. Life is only the mirror into which a man gazes not in order that he may get a reflection of himself, but that he may come to understand himself by that reflection; that he may see *what* it is that the mirror shows. Life is the proofsheet, in which the compositors' errors are brought to light. How they become visible, and whether the type is large or small, are matters of no consequence. Neither in the externals of life nor in the course of history is there any significance; for as it is all one whether an error occurs in the large type or in the small, so it is all one, as regards the essence of the matter, whether an evil disposition is mirrored as a conqueror of the world or a common swindler or ill-natured egoist. In one case he is seen of all men; in the other, perhaps only of himself; but that he should see himself is what signifies.

Therefore if egoism has a firm hold of a man and masters him, whether it be in the form of joy, or triumph, or lust, or hope, or frantic grief, or annoyance, or anger, or fear, or suspicion, or passion of any kind—he is in the devil's clutches and how he got into them does not matter. What is needful is that he should make haste to get out of them; and here, again, it does not matter how.

I have described *character* as *theoretically* an act of will lying beyond time, of which life in time, or *character in action,* is the development. For matters of practical life we all possess the one as well as the other; for we are constituted of them both. Character modifies our life more than we think, and it is to a certain extent true that every man is the architect of his own fortune. No doubt it seems as if our lot were assigned to us almost entirely from without, and imparted to us in something of the same way in which a melody outside us reaches the ear. But on looking back over our past, we see at once that our life consists of mere variations on one and the same theme, namely, our character, and that the same fundamental bass sounds through it all. This is an experience which a man can and must make in and by himself.

Not only a man's life, but his intellect too, may be possessed of a clear and definite character, so far as his intellect is applied to matters of theory. It is not every man, however, who has an intellect of this kind; for any such definite individuality as I mean is genius—an original view of the world, which presupposes an absolutely exceptional individuality, which is the essence of genius. A man's intellectual character is the theme on which all his works are variations. In an essay which I wrote in Weimar I called it the knack by which every genius produces his works, however various. This intellectual character determines the physiognomy of men of genius—what I might call *the theoretical physiognomy*—and gives it that distinguished expression which is chiefly seen in the eyes and the forehead. In the case of ordinary men the physiognomy presents no more than a weak analogy with the physiognomy of genius. On the other hand, all men possess *the practical physiognomy,* the stamp of will, of practical character, of moral disposition; and it shows itself chiefly in the mouth.

Since character, so far as we understand its nature, is above and beyond time, it cannot undergo any change under the influence of life. But although it must necessarily remain the same always, it requires time to unfold itself and show the very diverse aspects which it may possess. For character consists of two factors: one, the will-to-live itself, blind impulse, so-called impetuosity; the other, the restraint which the will acquires when it comes to understand the world; and the world, again, is itself will. A man may begin by following the craving of desire, until he comes to see how hollow and unreal a thing is life, how deceitful are its pleasures, what horrible aspects it possesses; and this it is that makes people hermits, penitents, Magdalenes. Nevertheless it is to be observed that no such change from a life of great indulgence in pleasure to one of resignation is possible, except to the man who of his own accord renounces pleasure. A really bad life cannot be changed into a virtuous one. The most beautiful soul, before it comes to know life from its horrible side, may eagerly drink the sweets of life and remain innocent. But it cannot commit a bad action; it cannot cause others suffering to do a pleasure to itself, for in that case it would see clearly what it would be doing; and whatever be its youth and inexperience it perceives the sufferings of others as clearly as its own pleasures. That is why one bad action is a guarantee that numberless others will be committed as soon as circumstances give occasion for them. Somebody once remarked to me, with entire justice, that every man had something very good and humane in his disposition, and also something very bad and malignant; and that according as he was moved one or the other of them made its appearance. The sight of others' suffering arouses, not only in different men, but in one and the same man, at one moment an inexhaustible sympathy, at another a certain satisfaction; and this satisfaction may increase until it becomes the

cruellest delight in pain. I observe in myself that at one moment I
regard all mankind with heartfelt pity, at another with the greatest
indifference, on occasion with hatred, nay, with a positive enjoyment of their pain.

All this shows very clearly that we are possessed of two different, nay, absolutely contradictory, ways of regarding the world:
one according to the principle of individuation, which exhibits
all creatures as entire strangers to us, as definitely not ourselves.
We can have no feelings for them but those of indifference, envy,
hatred, and delight that they suffer. The other way of regarding
the world is in accordance with what I may call the *Tat-twam-
asi*—*this-is-thyself* principle. All creatures are exhibited as identical
with ourselves; and so it is pity and love which the sight of them
arouses.

The one method separates individuals by impassable barriers;
the other removes the barrier and brings the individuals together.
The one makes us feel, in regard to every man, *that is what I am;*
the other, *that is not what I am.* But it is remarkable that while the
sight of another's suffering makes us feel our identity with him,
and arouses our pity, this is not so with the sight of another's happiness. Then we almost always feel some envy; and even though
we may have no such feeling in certain cases,—as, for instance,
when our friends are happy,—yet the interest which we take in
their happiness is of a weak description, and cannot compare with
the sympathy which we feel with their suffering. Is this because
we recognise all happiness to be a delusion, or an impediment to
true welfare? No! I am inclined to think that it is because the sight
of the pleasure, or the possessions, which are denied to us, arouses
envy; that is to say, the wish that we, and not the other, had that
pleasure or those possessions.

It is only the first way of looking at the world which is founded
on any demonstrable reason. The other is, as it were, the gate
out of this world; it has no attestation beyond itself, unless it be
the very abstract and difficult proof which my doctrine supplies.
Why the first way predominates in one man, and the second in
another—though perhaps it does not exclusively predominate in
any man; why the one or the other emerges according as the will

is moved—these are deep problems. The paths of night and day are close together:—

Ἐγγὺς γὰρ νυκτός δε καὶ ἤματος εἰσι κέλευθοι.

It is a fact that there is a great and original difference between one empirical character and another; and it is a difference which, at bottom, rests upon the relation of the individual's will to his intellectual faculty. This relation is finally determined by the degree of will in his father and of intellect in his mother; and the union of father and mother is for the most part an affair of chance. This would all mean a revolting injustice in the nature of the world, if it were not that the difference between parents and son is phenomenal only and all chance is, at bottom, necessity.

As regards the freedom of the will, if it were the case that the will manifested itself in a single act alone, it would be a free act. But the will manifests itself in a course of life, that is to say, in a series of acts. Every one of these acts, therefore, is determined as a part of a complete whole, and cannot happen otherwise than it does happen. On the other hand, the whole series is free; it is simply the manifestation of an individualised will.

If a man feels inclined to commit a bad action and refrains, he is kept back either (1) by fear of punishment or vengeance; or (2) by superstition in other words, fear of punishment in a future life; or (3) by the feeling of sympathy, including general charity; or (4) by the feeling of honour, in other words, the fear of shame; or (5) by the feeling of justice, that is, an objective attachment to fidelity and good-faith, coupled with a resolve to hold them sacred, because they are the foundation of all free intercourse between man and man, and therefore often of advantage to himself as well. This last thought, not indeed as a thought, but as a mere feeling, influences people very frequently. It is this that often compels a man of honour, when some great but unjust advantage is offered him, to reject it with contempt and proudly exclaim: *I am an honourable man!* For otherwise how should a poor man, confronted with the property which chance or even some worse agency has bestowed on the rich, whose very existence it is that makes him poor, feel so much sincere respect for this property, that he refuses to touch it even in his need; and although he has a prospect of escaping punishment, what other thought is it that can be at the bottom of such a man's honesty? He is resolved not to separate himself from the great community of honourable people who have the earth in possession, and whose laws are recognised everywhere. He knows that a single dishonest act will ostracise and proscribe him from that society for ever. No! a man will spend money on any soil that yields him good fruit, and he will make sacrifices for it.

With a good action,—that, every action in which a man's own advantage is ostensibly subordinated to another's,—the motive is either (1) self-interest, kept in the background; or (2) superstition, in other words, self-interest in the form of reward in another life; or (3) sympathy; or (4) the desire to lend a helping hand, in other words, attachment to the maxim that we should assist one another in need, and the wish to maintain this maxim, in view of the presumption that some day we ourselves may find it serve our turn. For what Kant calls a good action done from motives of duty and for the sake of duty, there is, as will be seen, no room at all. Kant himself declares it to be doubtful whether an action was ever determined by pure motives of duty alone. I affirm most certainly that no action was ever so done; it is mere babble; there is nothing in it that could really act as a motive to any man. When he shelters himself behind verbiage of that sort, he is always actuated by one of the four motives which I have described. Among these it is obviously sympathy alone which is quite genuine and sincere.

Good and *bad* apply to character only *à potiori;* that is to say, we prefer the good to the bad; but, absolutely, there is no such distinction. The difference arises at the point which lies between subordinating one's own advantage to that of another, and not subordinating it. If a man keeps to the exact middle, he is *just.* But most men go an inch in their regard for others' welfare to twenty yards in regard for their own.

The source of *good* and of *bad character,* so far as we have any real knowledge of it, lies in this, that with the bad character the thought of the external world, and especially of the living creatures in it, is accompanied—all the more, the greater the resemblance between them and the individual self—by a constant feeling of *not I, not I, not I.*

Contrarily, with the good character (both being assumed to exist in a high degree) the same thought has for its accompaniment, like a fundamental bass, a constant feeling of *I, I, I.* From this spring benevolence and a disposition to help all men, and at the same time a cheerful, confident and tranquil frame of mind, the opposite of that which accompanies the bad character.

The difference, however, is only phenomenal, although it is a difference which is radical. But now we come to the *hardest of all problems:* How is it that, while the will, as the thing-in-itself, is identical, and from a metaphysical point of view one and the same in all its manifestations, there is nevertheless such an enormous difference between one character and another?—the malicious, diabolical wickedness of the one, and set off against it, the goodness of the other, showing all the more conspicuously. How is it that we get a Tiberius, a Caligula, a Carcalla, a Domitian, a Nero; and on the other hand, the Antonines, Titus, Hadrian, Nerva? How is it that among the animals, nay, in a higher species, in individual animals, there is a like difference?—the malignity of the cat most strongly developed in the tiger; the spite of the monkey; on the other hand, goodness, fidelity and love in the dog and the elephant. It is obvious that the principle of wickedness in the brute is the same as in man.

We may to some extent modify the difficulty of the problem by observing that the whole difference is in the end only one of degree. In every living creature, the fundamental propensities and instincts all exist, but they exist in very different degrees and proportions. This, however, is not enough to explain the facts.

We must fall back upon the intellect and its relation to the will; it is the only explanation that remains. A man's intellect, however, by no means stands in any direct and obvious relation with the goodness of his character. We may, it is true, discriminate between two kinds of intellect: between understanding, as the apprehension of relation in accordance with the Principle of Sufficient Reason, and cognition, a faculty akin to genius, which acts more directly, is independent of this law, and passes beyond the Principle of Individuation. The latter is the faculty which apprehends Ideas, and it is the faculty which has to do with morality. But even this explanation leaves much to be desired. *Fine minds are seldom fine souls* was the correct observation of Jean Paul; although they are never the contrary. Lord Bacon, who, to be sure, was less a fine soul than a fine mind, was a scoundrel.

I have declared space and time to be part of the Principle of Individuation, as it is only space and time that make the multiplicity of similar objects a possibility. But multiplicity itself also admits of variety; multiplicity and diversity are not only quantitative, but also qualitative. How is it that there is such a thing as qualitative diversity, especially in ethical matters? Or have I fallen into an error the opposite of that in which Leibnitz fell with his *identitas indiscernibilium?*

The chief cause of intellectual diversity is to be found in the brain and nervous system. This is a fact which somewhat lessens the obscurity of the subject. With the brutes the intellect and the brain are strictly adapted to their aims and needs. With man alone there is now and then, by way of exception, a superfluity, which, if it is abundant, may yield genius. But ethical diversity, it seems, proceeds immediately from the will. Otherwise ethical character would not be above and beyond time, as it is only in the individual that intellect and will are united. The will is above and beyond time, and eternal; and character is innate; that is to say, it is sprung from the same eternity, and therefore it does not admit of any but a transcendental explanation.

Perhaps some one will come after me who will throw light into this dark abyss.

Moral Instinct

An act done by instinct differs from every other kind of act in that an understanding of its object does not precede it but follows upon it. Instinct is therefore a rule of action given *à priori*. We may be unaware of the object to which it is directed, as no understanding of it is necessary to its attainment. On the other hand, if an act is done by an exercise of reason or intelligence, it proceeds according to a rule which the understanding has itself devised for the purpose of carrying out a preconceived aim. Hence it is that action according to rule may miss its aim, while instinct is infallible.

On the *à priori* character of instinct we may compare what Plato says in the *Philebus*. With Plato instinct is a reminiscence of something which a man has never actually experienced in his lifetime; in the same way as, in the *Phædo* and elsewhere, everything that a man learns is regarded as a reminiscence. He has no other word to express the *à priori* element in all experience.

There are, then, three things that are *à priori*:—

(1) Theoretical Reason, in other words, the conditions which make all experience possible.

(2) Instinct, or the rule by which an object promoting the life of the senses may, though unknown, be attained.

(3) The Moral Law, or the rule by which an action takes place without any object.

Accordingly rational or intelligent action proceeds by a rule laid down in accordance with the object as it is understood. Instinctive action proceeds by a rule without an understanding of the object of it. Moral action proceeds by a rule without any object at all.

Theoretical Reason is the aggregate of rules in accordance with which all my knowledge—that is to say, the whole world of experience—necessarily proceeds. In the same manner *Instinct* is the aggregate of rules in accordance with which all my action necessarily proceeds if it meets with no obstruction. Hence it seems to me that Instinct may most appropriately be called *practical reason,* for like theoretical reason it determines the *must* of all experience.

The so-called moral law, on the other hand, is only one aspect of *the better consciousness,* the aspect which it presents from the point of view of instinct. This better consciousness is something lying beyond all experience, that is, beyond all reason, whether of the theoretical or the practical kind, and has nothing to do with it; whilst it is in virtue of the mysterious union of it and reason in the same individual that the better consciousness comes into conflict with reason, leaving the individual to choose between the two.

In any conflict between the better consciousness and reason, if the individual decides for reason, should it be theoretical reason, he becomes a narrow, pedantic philistine; should it be practical, a rascal.

If he decides for the better consciousness, we can make no further positive affirmation about him, for if we were to do so, we should find ourselves in the realm of reason; and as it is only what takes place within this realm that we can speak of at all it follows that we cannot speak of the better consciousness except in negative terms.

This shows us how it is that reason is hindered and obstructed; that *theoretical reason* is suppressed in favour of *genius,* and *practical reason* in favour of *virtue.* Now the better consciousness is neither theoretical nor practical; for these are distinctions that only apply to reason. But if the individual is in the act of choosing, the better consciousness appears to him in the aspect which it assumes in vanquishing and overcoming the practical reason (or instinct, to use the common word). It appears to him as an imperative command, an *ought.* It so appears to him, I say; in other words, that is the shape which it takes for the theoretical reason which renders all things into objects and ideas. But in so far as the better consciousness desires to vanquish and overcome the theoretical reason, it takes no shape at all; on the simple ground that, as it comes into play, the theoretical reason is suppressed and becomes the mere servant of the better consciousness. That is why genius can never give any account of its own works.

In the morality of action, the legal principle that both sides are to be heard must not be allowed to apply; in other words, the claims of self and the senses must not be urged. Nay, on the contrary, as soon as the pure will has found expression, the case is closed; *nec audienda altera pars.*

The lower animals are not endowed with moral freedom. Probably this is not because they show no trace of the better consciousness which in us is manifested as morality, or nothing analogous to it; for, if that were so, the lower animals, which are in so many respects like ourselves in outward appearance that we regard man as a species of animal, would possess some *raison d'être* entirely different from our own, and actually be, in their essential and inmost nature, something quite other than ourselves. This is a contention which is obviously refuted by the thoroughly malignant and inherently vicious character of certain animals, such as the crocodile, the hyæna, the scorpion, the snake, and the gentle, affectionate and contented character of others, such as the dog. Here, as in the case of men, the character, as it is manifested, must rest upon something that is above and beyond time. For, as Jacob Böhme says,[1] *there is a power in every animal which is indestructible, and the spirit of the world draws it into itself, against the final separation at the Last Judgment.* Therefore we cannot call the lower animals free, and the reason why we cannot do so is that they are wanting in a faculty which is profoundly subordinate to the better consciousness in its highest phase, I mean reason. Reason is the faculty of supreme comprehension, the idea of totality. How reason manifests itself in the theoretical sphere Kant has shown, and it does the same in the practical: it makes us capable of observing and surveying the whole of our life, thought, and action, in continual connection, and therefore of acting according to general maxims, whether those maxims originate in the understanding as prudential rules, or in the better consciousness as moral laws.

---

[1] *Epistles,* 56.

If any desire or passion is aroused in us, we, and in the same way the lower animals, are for the moment filled with this desire; we are all anger, all lust, all fear; and in such moments neither the better consciousness can speak, nor the understanding consider the consequences. But in our case reason allows us even at that moment to see our actions and our life as an unbroken chain,—a chain which connects our earlier resolutions, or, it may be, the future consequences of our action, with the moment of passion which now fills our whole consciousness. It shows us the identity of our person, even when that person is exposed to influences of the most varied kind, and thereby we are enabled to act according to maxims. The lower animal is wanting in this faculty; the passion which seizes it completely dominates it, and can be checked only by another passion—anger, for instance, or lust, by fear; even though the vision that terrifies does not appeal to the senses, but is present in the animal only as a dim memory and imagination. Men, therefore, may be called irrational, if, like the lower animals, they allow themselves to be determined by the moment.

So far, however, is reason from being the source of morality that it is reason alone which makes us capable of being rascals, which the lower animals cannot be. It is reason which enables us to form an evil resolution and to keep it when the provocation to evil is removed; it enables us, for example, to nurse vengeance. Although at the moment that we have an opportunity of fulfilling our resolution the better consciousness may manifest itself as love or charity, it is by force of reason, in pursuance of some evil maxim, that we act against it. Thus Goethe says that a man may use his reason only for the purpose of being more bestial than any beast:—

> *Er hat Vernunft, doch braucht er sie allein*
> *Um theirischer als jedes Thier zu sein.*

For not only do we, like the beasts, satisfy the desires of the moment, but we refine upon them and stimulate them in order to prepare the desire for the satisfaction.

Whenever we think that we perceive a trace of reason in the lower animals, it fills us with surprise. Now our surprise is not excited by the good and affectionate disposition which some of them exhibit—we recognise that as something other than reason—but by some action in them which seems to be determined not by the impression of the moment but by a resolution previously made and kept. Elephants, for instance, are reported to have taken premeditated revenge for insults long after they were suffered; lions, to have requited benefits on an opportunity tardily offered. The truth of such stories has, however, no bearing at all on the question, What do we mean by reason? But they enable us to decide whether in the lower animals there is any trace of anything that we can call reason.

Kant not only declares that all our moral sentiments originate in reason, but he lays down that reason, *in my sense of the word*, is a condition of moral action; as he holds that for an action to be virtuous and meritorious it must be done in accordance with maxims, and not spring from a resolve taken under some momentary impression. But in both contentions he is wrong. If I resolve to take vengeance on some one, and when an opportunity offers, the better consciousness in the form of love and humanity speaks its word, and I am influenced by it rather than by my evil resolution, this is a virtuous act, for it is a manifestation of the better consciousness. It is possible to conceive of a very virtuous man in whom the better consciousness is so continuously active that it is never silent, and never allows his passions to get a complete hold of him. By such consciousness he is subject to a direct control, instead of being guided indirectly, through the medium of reason, by means of maxims and moral principles. That is why a man may have weak reasoning powers and a weak understanding and yet have a high sense of morality and be eminently good; for the most important element in a man depends as little on intellectual as it does on physical strength. Jesus says, *Blessed are the poor in spirit*. And Jacob Böhme has the excellent and noble observation: *Whoso lies quietly in his own will, like a child in the womb, and lets himself be led and guided by that inner principle from which he is sprung, is the noblest and richest on earth.*[1]

---

[1] *Epistles*, 37.

Ethical Reflections

The philosophers of the ancient world united in a single conception a great many things that had no connection with one another. Of this every dialogue of Plato's furnishes abundant examples. The greatest and worst confusion of this kind is that between ethics and politics. The State and the Kingdom of God, or the Moral Law, are so entirely different in their character that the former is a parody of the latter, a bitter mockery at the absence of it. Compared with the Moral Law the State is a crutch instead of a limb, an automaton instead of a man.

★ ★ ★ ★ ★

The *principle of honour* stands in close connection with human freedom. It is, as it were, an abuse of that freedom. Instead of using his freedom to fulfil the moral law, a man employs his power of voluntarily undergoing any feeling of pain, of overcoming any momentary impression, in order that he may assert his self-will, whatever be the object to which he directs it. As he thereby shows that, unlike the lower animals, he has thoughts which go beyond the welfare of his body and whatever makes for that welfare, it has come about that the principle of honour is often confused with virtue. They are regarded as if they were twins. But wrongly; for although the principle of honour is something which distinguishes man from the lower animals, it is not, in itself, anything that raises him above them. Taken as an end and aim, it is as dark a delusion as any other aim that springs from self. Used as a means, or casually, it may be productive of good; but even that is good which is vain and frivolous. It is the misuse of freedom, the employment of it as a weapon for overcoming the world of feeling, that makes man so infinitely more terrible than the lower animals; for they do only what momentary instinct bids them; while man acts by ideas, and his ideas may entail universal ruin before they are satisfied.

There is another circumstance which helps to promote the notion that honour and virtue are connected. A man who can do what he wants to do shows that he can also do it if what he wants to do is a virtuous act. But that those of our actions which we are ourselves obliged to regard with contempt are also regarded with contempt by other people serves more than anything that I have here mentioned to establish the connection. Thus it often happens that a man who is not afraid of the one kind of contempt is unwilling to undergo the other. But when we are called upon to choose between our own approval and the world's censure, as may occur in complicated and mistaken circumstances, what becomes of the principle of honour then?

Two characteristic examples of the principle of honour are to be found in Shakespeare's *Henry VI.,* Part II., Act IV., Sc. 1. A pirate is anxious to murder his captive instead of accepting, like others, a ransom for him; because in taking his captive he lost an eye, and his own honour and that of his forefathers would in his opinion be stained, if he were to allow his revenge to be bought off as though he were a mere trader. The prisoner, on the other hand, who is the Duke of Suffolk, prefers to have his head grace a pole than to uncover it to such a low fellow as a pirate, by approaching him to ask for mercy.

Just as civic honour—in other words, the opinion that we deserve to be trusted—is the palladium of those whose endeavour it is to make their way in the world on the path of honourable business, so knightly honour—in other words, the opinion that we are men to be feared—is the palladium of those who aim at going through life on the path of violence; and so it was that knightly honour arose among the robber-knights and other knights of the Middle Ages.

★ ★ ★ ★ ★

A theoretical philosopher is one who can supply in the shape of ideas for the reason, a copy of the presentations of experience;

just as what the painter sees he can reproduce on canvas; the sculp-
tor, in marble; the poet, in pictures for the imagination, though
they are pictures which he supplies only in sowing the ideas from
which they sprang.

A so-called practical philosopher, on the other hand, is one
who, contrarily, deduces his action from ideas. The theoretical
philosopher transforms life into ideas. The practical philosopher
transforms ideas into life; he acts, therefore, in a thoroughly reasonable manner; he is consistent, regular, deliberate; he is never
hasty or passionate; he never allows himself to be influenced by the
impression of the moment.

And indeed, when we find ourselves among those full presentations of experience, or real objects, to which the body belongs—
since the body is only an objectified will, the shape which the
will assumes in the material world—it is difficult to let our bodies
be guided, not by those presentations, but by a mere image of
them, by cold, colourless ideas, which are related to experience
as the shadow of Orcus to life; and yet this is the only way in
which we can avoid doing things of which we may have to
repent.

The theoretical philosopher enriches the domain of reason by
adding to it; the practical philosopher draws upon it, and makes it
serve him.

★ ★ ★ ★ ★

According to Kant the truth of experience is only a hypotheti-
cal truth. If the suppositions which underlie all the intimations
of experience—subject, object, time, space and causality—were
removed, none of those intimations would contain a word of truth.
In other words, experience is only a phenomenon; it is not knowledge of the thing-in-itself.

If we find something in our own conduct at which we are
secretly pleased, although we cannot reconcile it with experience,
seeing that if we were to follow the guidance of experience we
should have to do precisely the opposite, we must not allow this
to put us out; otherwise we should be ascribing an authority to
experience which it does not deserve, for all that it teaches rests

upon a mere supposition. This is the general tendency of the Kantian Ethics.

★ ★ ★ ★ ★

Innocence is in its very nature stupid. It is stupid because the aim of life (I use the expression only figuratively, and I could just as well speak of the essence of life, or of the world) is to gain a knowledge of our own bad will, so that our will may become an object for us, and that we may undergo an inward conversion. Our body is itself our will objectified; it is one of the first and foremost of objects, and the deeds that we accomplish for the sake of the body show us the evil inherent in our will. In the state of innocence, where there is no evil because there is no experience, man is, as it were, only an apparatus for living, and the object for which the apparatus exists is not yet disclosed. An empty form of life like this, a stage untenanted, is in itself, like the so-called real world, null and void; and as it can attain a meaning only by action, by error, by knowledge, by the convulsions of the will, it wears a character of insipid stupidity. A golden age of innocence, a fools' paradise, is a notion that is stupid and unmeaning, and for that very reason in no way worthy of any respect. The first criminal and murderer, Cain, who acquired a knowledge of guilt, and through guilt acquired a knowledge of virtue by repentance, and so came to understand the meaning of life, is a tragical figure more significant, and almost more respectable, than all the innocent fools in the world put together.

★ ★ ★ ★ ★

If I had to write about *modesty* I should say: I know the esteemed public for which I have the honour to write far too well to dare to give utterance to my opinion about this virtue. Personally I am quite content to be modest and to apply myself to this virtue with the utmost possible circumspection. But one thing I shall never admit—that I have ever required modesty of any man, and any statement to that effect I repel as a slander.

The paltry character of most men compels the few who have any merit or genius to behave as though they did not know their own value, and consequently did not know other people's want of value; for it is only on this condition that the mob acquiesces in tolerating merit. A virtue has been made out of this necessity, and it is called modesty. It is a piece of hypocrisy, to be excused only because other people are so paltry that they must be treated with indulgence.

★ ★ ★ ★ ★

Human misery may affect us in two ways, and we may be in one of two opposite moods in regard to it.

In one of them, this misery is immediately present to us. We feel it in our own person, in our own will which, imbued with violent desires, is everywhere broken, and this is the process which constitutes suffering. The result is that the will increases in violence, as is shown in all cases of passion and emotion; and this increasing violence comes to a stop only when the will turns and gives way to complete resignation, in other words, is redeemed. The man who is entirely dominated by this mood will regard any prosperity which he may see in others with envy, and any suffering with no sympathy.

In the opposite mood human misery is present to us only as a fact of knowledge, that is to say, indirectly. We are mainly engaged in looking at the sufferings of others, and our attention is withdrawn from our own. It is in their person that we become aware of human misery; we are filled with sympathy; and the result of this mood is general benevolence, philanthropy. All envy vanishes, and instead of feeling it, we are rejoiced when we see one of our tormented fellow-creatures experience any pleasure or relief.

After the same fashion we may be in one of two opposite moods in regard to human baseness and depravity. In the one we perceive this baseness indirectly, in others. Out of this mood arise indignation, hatred, and contempt of mankind. In the other we perceive it directly, in ourselves. Out of it there arises humiliation, nay, contrition.

In order to judge the moral value of a man, it is very important to observe which of these four moods predominate in him. They go in pairs, one out of each division. In very excellent characters the second mood of each division will predominate.

★ ★ ★ ★ ★

The categorical imperative, or absolute command, is a contradiction. Every command is conditional. What is unconditional and necessary is a *must,* such as is presented by the laws of nature.

It is quite true that the moral law is entirely conditional. There is a world and a view of life in which it has neither validity nor significance. That world is, properly speaking, the real world in which, as individuals, we live; for every regard paid to morality is a denial of that world and of our individual life in it. It is a view of the world, however, which does not go beyond the principle of sufficient reason; and the opposite view proceeds by the intuition of Ideas.

★ ★ ★ ★ ★

If a man is under the influence of two opposite but very strong motives, A and B, and I am greatly concerned that he should choose A, but still more that he should never be untrue to his choice, and by changing his mind betray me, or the like, it will not do for me to say anything that might hinder the motive B from having its full effect upon him, and only emphasise A; for then I should never be able to reckon on his decision. What I have to do is, rather, to put both motives before him at the same time, in as vivid and clear a way as possible, so that they may work upon him with their whole force. The choice that he then makes is the decision of his inmost nature, and stands firm to all eternity. In saying *I will do this,* he has said *I must do this.* I have got at his will, and I can rely upon its working as steadily as one of the forces of nature. It is as certain as fire kindles and water wets that he will act according to the motive which has proved to be stronger for him. Insight and knowledge may be attained and lost again; they may be changed, or improved, or destroyed; but will cannot be changed. That is why *I apprehend, I perceive, I see,* is subject to alteration and uncertainty; *I will,* pronounced on a right apprehension of motive, is as firm as nature itself.

The difficulty, however, lies in getting at a right apprehension. A man's apprehension of motive may change, or be corrected or perverted; and on the other hand, his circumstances may undergo an alteration.

★ ★ ★ ★ ★

A man should exercise an almost boundless toleration and placability, because if he is capricious enough to refuse to forgive a single individual for the meanness or evil that lies at his door, it is doing the rest of the world a quite unmerited honour.

But at the same time the man who is every one's friend is no one's friend. It is quite obvious what sort of friendship it is which we hold out to the human race, and to which it is open to almost every man to return, no matter what he may have done.

★ ★ ★ ★ ★

With the ancients *friendship* was one of the chief elements in morality. But friendship is only limitation and partiality; it is the restriction to one individual of what is the due of all mankind, namely, the recognition that a man's own nature and that of mankind are identical. At most it is a compromise between this recognition and selfishness.

★ ★ ★ ★ ★

A lie always has its origin in the desire to extend the dominion of one's own will over other individuals, and to deny their will in order the better to affirm one's own. Consequently a lie is in its very nature the product of injustice, malevolence and villainy. That is why truth, sincerity, candour and rectitude are at once recognised and valued as praiseworthy and noble qualities; because we presume that the man who exhibits them entertains no sentiments of injustice or malice, and therefore stands in no need of concealing such sentiments. He who is open cherishes nothing that is bad.

★ ★ ★ ★ ★

There is a certain kind of courage which springs from the same source as good-nature. What I mean is that the good-natured man is almost as clearly conscious that he exists in other individuals as in himself. I have often shown how this feeling gives rise to good-nature. It also gives rise to courage, for the simple reason that the man who possesses this feeling cares less for his own individual existence, as he lives almost as much in the general existence of all creatures. Accordingly he is little concerned for his own life and its belongings. This is by no means the sole source of courage for it is a phenomenon due to various causes. But it is the noblest kind of courage, as is shown by the fact that in its origin it is associated with great gentleness and patience. Men of this kind are usually irresistible to women.

* * * * *

All general rules and precepts fail, because they proceed from the false assumption that men are constituted wholly, or almost wholly, alike; an assumption which the philosophy of Helvetius expressly makes. Whereas the truth is that the original difference between individuals in intellect and morality is immeasurable.

* * * * *

The question as to whether morality is something real is the question whether a well-grounded counter-principle to egoism actually exists.

As egoism restricts concern for welfare to a single individual, *viz.,* the man's own self, the counter-principle would have to extend it to all other individuals.

* * * * *

It is only because the will is above and beyond time that the stings of conscience are ineradicable, and do not, like other pains, gradually wear away. No! an evil deed weighs on the conscience years afterwards as heavily as if it had been freshly committed.

* * * * *

Character is innate, and conduct is merely its manifestation; the occasion for great misdeeds comes seldom; strong counter-motives keep us back; our disposition is revealed to ourselves by our desires, thoughts, emotions, when it remains unknown to others. Reflecting on all this, we might suppose it possible for a man to possess, in some sort, an innate evil conscience, without ever having done anything very bad.

★ ★ ★ ★ ★

Don't do to others what you wouldn't like done to yourself. This is, perhaps, one of those arguments that prove, or rather ask, too much. For a prisoner might address it to a judge.

★ ★ ★ ★ ★

Stupid people are generally malicious, for the very same reason as the ugly and the deformed.

Similarly, genius and sanctity are akin. However simple-minded a saint may be, he will nevertheless have a dash of genius in him; and however many errors of temperament, or of actual character, a genius may possess, he will still exhibit a certain nobility of disposition by which he shows his kinship with the saint.

★ ★ ★ ★ ★

The great difference between Law without and Law within, between the State and the Kingdom of God, is very clear. It is the State's business to see that *every one should have justice done to him;* it regards men as passive beings, and therefore takes no account of anything but their actions. The Moral Law, on the other hand, is concerned that *every one should do justice;* it regards men as active, and looks to the will rather than the deed. To prove that this is the true distinction let the reader consider what would happen if he were to say, conversely, that it is the State's business that every one should do justice, and the business of the Moral Law that every one should have justice done to him. The absurdity is obvious.

As an example of the distinction, let me take the case of a debtor and a creditor disputing about a debt which the former denies. A lawyer and a moralist are present, and show a lively interest in the matter. Both desire that the dispute should end in the same way, although what they want is by no means the same. The lawyer says, *I want this man to get back what belongs to him;* and the moralist, *I want that man to do his duty.*

It is with the will alone that morality is concerned. Whether external force hinders or fails to hinder the will from working does not in the least matter. For morality the external world is real only in so far as it is able or unable to lead and influence the will. As soon as the will is determined, that is, as soon as a resolve is taken, the external world and its events are of no further moment and practically do not exist. For if the events of the world had any such reality—that is to say, if they possessed a significance in themselves, or any other than that derived from the will which is affected by them—what a grievance it would be that all these events lie in the realm of chance and error! It is, however, just this which proves that the important thing is not what happens, but what is willed. Accordingly, let the incidents of life be left to the play of chance and error, to demonstrate to man that he is as chaff before the wind.

The State concerns itself only with the incidents—with what happens; nothing else has any reality for it. I may dwell upon thoughts of murder and poison as much as I please: the State does not forbid me, so long as the axe and rope control my will, and prevent it from becoming action.

Ethics asks: What are the duties towards others which justice imposes upon us? in other words, What must I render? The Law of Nature asks: What need I not submit to from others? that is, What must I suffer? The question is put, not that I may do no injustice, but that I may not do more than every man must do if he is to safeguard his existence, and than every man will approve being done, in order that he may be treated in the same way himself; and, further, that I may not do more than society will permit me to do. The same answer will serve for both questions, just as the same straight line can be drawn from either of two opposite directions, namely, by opposing forces; or, again, as the angle can give the sine, or the sine the angle.

It has been said that the historian is an inverted prophet. In the same way it may be said that a teacher of law is an inverted moralist (*viz.*, a teacher of the duties of justice), or that politics are inverted ethics, if we exclude the thought that ethics also teaches the duty of benevolence, magnanimity, love, and so on. The State is the Gordian knot that is cut instead of being untied; it is Columbus' egg which is made to stand by being broken instead of balanced, as though the business in question were to make it stand rather than to balance it. In this respect the State is like the man who thinks that he can produce fine weather by making the barometer go up.

★ ★ ★ ★ ★

The pseudo-philosophers of our age tell us that it is the object of the State to promote the moral aims of mankind. This is not true; it is rather the contrary which is true. The aim for which mankind exists—the expression is parabolic—is not that a man should act in such and such a manner; for all *opera operata,* things that have actually been done, are in themselves matters of indifference. No! the aim is that the Will, of which every man is a complete specimen—nay, is the very Will itself—should turn whither it needs to turn; that the man himself (the union of Thought and Will) should perceive what this will is, and what horrors it contains; that he should show the reflection of himself in his own deeds, in the abomination of them. The State, which is wholly concerned with the general welfare, checks the manifestation of the bad will, but in no wise checks the will itself; the attempt would be impossible. It is because the State checks the manifestation of his will that a man very seldom sees the whole abomination of his nature in the mirror of his deeds. Or does the reader actually suppose there are no people in the world as bad as Robespierre, Napoleon, or other murderers? Does he fail to see that there are many who would act like them if only they could?

Many a criminal dies more quietly on the scaffold than many a non-criminal in the arms of his family. The one has perceived what his will is and has discarded it. The other has not been able to discard it, because he has never been able to perceive what it is. The aim of the State is to produce a fool's paradise, and this is in direct conflict with the true aim of life, namely, to attain a knowledge of what the will, in its horrible nature, really is.

★ ★ ★ ★ ★

Napoleon was not really worse than many, not to say most, men. He was possessed of the very ordinary egoism that seeks its welfare at the expense of others. What distinguished him was merely the greater power he had of satisfying his will, and greater intelligence, reason and courage; added to which, chance gave him a favourable scope for his operations. By means of all this he did for his egoism what a thousand other men would like to do for theirs, but cannot. Every feeble lad who by little acts of villainy gains a small advantage for himself by putting others to some disadvantage, although it may be equally small, is just as bad as Napoleon.

Those who fancy that retribution comes after death would demand that Napoleon should by unutterable torments pay the penalty for all the numberless calamities that he caused. But he is no more culpable than all those who possess the same will, unaccompanied by the same power.

The circumstance that in his case this extraordinary power was added allowed him to reveal the whole wickedness of the human will; and the sufferings of his age, as the necessary obverse of the medal, reveal the misery which is inextricably bound up with this bad will. It is the general manipulation of this will that constitutes the world. But it is precisely that it should be understood how inextricably the will to live is bound up with, and is really one and the same as, this unspeakable misery, that is the world's aim and purpose; and it is an aim and purpose which the appearance of Napoleon did much to assist. Not to be an unmeaning fools' paradise but a tragedy, in which the will to live understands itself and yields—that is the object for which the world exists. Napoleon is only an enormous mirror of the will to live.

The difference between the man who causes suffering and the man who suffers it, is only phenomenal. It is all a will to live, identical with great suffering; and it is only by understanding this that the will can mend and end.

★ ★ ★ ★ ★

What chiefly distinguishes ancient from modern times is that in ancient times, to use Napoleon's expression, it was affairs that reigned: *les paroles aux choses.* In modern times this is not so. What I mean is that in ancient times the character of public life, of the State, and of Religion, as well as of private life, was a strenuous affirmation of the will to live. In modern times it is a denial of this will, for such is the character of Christianity. But now while on the one hand that denial has suffered some abatement even in public opinion, because it is too repugnant to human character, on the other what is publicly denied is secretly affirmed. Hence it is that we see half measures and falsehood everywhere; and that is why modern times look so small beside antiquity.

★ ★ ★ ★ ★

The structure of human society is like a pendulum swinging between two impulses, two evils in polar opposition, *despotism* and *anarchy*. The further it gets from the one, the nearer it approaches the other. From this the reader might hit on the thought that if it were exactly midway between the two, it would be right. Far from it. For these two evils are by no means equally bad and dangerous. The former is incomparably less to be feared; its ills exist in the main only as possibilities, and if they come at all it is only one among millions that they touch. But, with anarchy, possibility and actuality are inseparable; its blows fall on every man every day. Therefore every constitution should be a nearer approach to a despotism than to anarchy; nay, it must contain a small possibility of despotism.

A CATALOG OF SELECTED
DOVER BOOKS
IN ALL FIELDS OF INTEREST

A CATALOG OF SELECTED DOVER
BOOKS IN ALL FIELDS OF INTEREST

100 BEST-LOVED POEMS, Edited by Philip Smith. "The Passionate Shepherd to His Love," "Shall I compare thee to a summer's day?" "Death, be not proud," "The Raven," "The Road Not Taken," plus works by Blake, Wordsworth, Byron, Shelley, Keats, many others. 96pp. 5³⁄₁₆ x 8¼.   0-486-28553-7

100 SMALL HOUSES OF THE THIRTIES, Brown-Blodgett Company. Exterior photographs and floor plans for 100 charming structures. Illustrations of models accompanied by descriptions of interiors, color schemes, closet space, and other amenities. 200 illustrations. 112pp. 8⅜ x 11.   0-486-44131-8

1000 TURN-OF-THE-CENTURY HOUSES: With Illustrations and Floor Plans, Herbert C. Chivers. Reproduced from a rare edition, this showcase of homes ranges from cottages and bungalows to sprawling mansions. Each house is meticulously illustrated and accompanied by complete floor plans. 256pp. 9⅜ x 12¼.
                                                                         0-486-45596-3

101 GREAT AMERICAN POEMS, Edited by The American Poetry & Literacy Project. Rich treasury of verse from the 19th and 20th centuries includes works by Edgar Allan Poe, Robert Frost, Walt Whitman, Langston Hughes, Emily Dickinson, T. S. Eliot, other notables. 96pp. 5³⁄₁₆ x 8¼.   0-486-40158-8

101 GREAT SAMURAI PRINTS, Utagawa Kuniyoshi. Kuniyoshi was a master of the warrior woodblock print — and these 18th-century illustrations represent the pinnacle of his craft. Full-color portraits of renowned Japanese samurais pulse with movement, passion, and remarkably fine detail. 112pp. 8⅜ x 11.   0-486-46523-3

ABC OF BALLET, Janet Grosser. Clearly worded, abundantly illustrated little guide defines basic ballet-related terms: arabesque, battement, pas de chat, relevé, sissonne, many others. Pronunciation guide included. Excellent primer. 48pp. 4³⁄₁₆ x 5¾.
                                                                         0-486-40871-X

ACCESSORIES OF DRESS: An Illustrated Encyclopedia, Katherine Lester and Bess Viola Oerke. Illustrations of hats, veils, wigs, cravats, shawls, shoes, gloves, and other accessories enhance an engaging commentary that reveals the humor and charm of the many-sided story of accessorized apparel. 644 figures and 59 plates. 608pp. 6 ⅛ x 9¼.
                                                                         0-486-43378-1

ADVENTURES OF HUCKLEBERRY FINN, Mark Twain. Join Huck and Jim as their boyhood adventures along the Mississippi River lead them into a world of excitement, danger, and self-discovery. Humorous narrative, lyrical descriptions of the Mississippi valley, and memorable characters. 224pp. 5³⁄₁₆ x 8¼.   0-486-28061-6

ALICE STARMORE'S BOOK OF FAIR ISLE KNITTING, Alice Starmore. A noted designer from the region of Scotland's Fair Isle explores the history and techniques of this distinctive, stranded-color knitting style and provides copious illustrated instructions for 14 original knitwear designs. 208pp. 8⅜ x 10⅞.   0-486-47218-3

CATALOG OF DOVER BOOKS

ALICE'S ADVENTURES IN WONDERLAND, Lewis Carroll. Beloved classic about a little girl lost in a topsy-turvy land and her encounters with the White Rabbit, March Hare, Mad Hatter, Cheshire Cat, and other delightfully improbable characters. 42 illustrations by Sir John Tenniel. 96pp. 5³⁄₁₆ x 8¼. 0-486-27543-4

AMERICA'S LIGHTHOUSES: An Illustrated History, Francis Ross Holland. Profusely illustrated fact-filled survey of American lighthouses since 1716. Over 200 stations — East, Gulf, and West coasts, Great Lakes, Hawaii, Alaska, Puerto Rico, the Virgin Islands, and the Mississippi and St. Lawrence Rivers. 240pp. 8 x 10¾. 0-486-25576-X

AN ENCYCLOPEDIA OF THE VIOLIN, Alberto Bachmann. Translated by Frederick H. Martens. Introduction by Eugene Ysaye. First published in 1925, this renowned reference remains unsurpassed as a source of essential information, from construction and evolution to repertoire and technique. Includes a glossary and 73 illustrations. 496pp. 6⅛ x 9¼. 0-486-46618-3

ANIMALS: 1,419 Copyright-Free Illustrations of Mammals, Birds, Fish, Insects, etc., Selected by Jim Harter. Selected for its visual impact and ease of use, this outstanding collection of wood engravings presents over 1,000 species of animals in extremely lifelike poses. Includes mammals, birds, reptiles, amphibians, fish, insects, and other invertebrates. 284pp. 9 x 12. 0-486-23766-4

THE ANNALS, Tacitus. Translated by Alfred John Church and William Jackson Brodribb. This vital chronicle of Imperial Rome, written by the era's great historian, spans A.D. 14-68 and paints incisive psychological portraits of major figures, from Tiberius to Nero. 416pp. 5³⁄₁₆ x 8¼. 0-486-45236-0

ANTIGONE, Sophocles. Filled with passionate speeches and sensitive probing of moral and philosophical issues, this powerful and often-performed Greek drama reveals the grim fate that befalls the children of Oedipus. Footnotes. 64pp. 5³⁄₁₆ x 8 ¼. 0-486-27804-2

ART DECO DECORATIVE PATTERNS IN FULL COLOR, Christian Stoll. Reprinted from a rare 1910 portfolio, 160 sensuous and exotic images depict a breathtaking array of florals, geometrics, and abstracts — all elegant in their stark simplicity. 64pp. 8⅜ x 11. 0-486-44862-2

THE ARTHUR RACKHAM TREASURY: 86 Full-Color Illustrations, Arthur Rackham. Selected and Edited by Jeff A. Menges. A stunning treasury of 86 full-page plates span the famed English artist's career, from *Rip Van Winkle* (1905) to masterworks such as *Undine, A Midsummer Night's Dream*, and *Wind in the Willows* (1939). 96pp. 8⅜ x 11. 0-486-44685-9

THE AUTHENTIC GILBERT & SULLIVAN SONGBOOK, W. S. Gilbert and A. S. Sullivan. The most comprehensive collection available, this songbook includes selections from every one of Gilbert and Sullivan's light operas. Ninety-two numbers are presented uncut and unedited, and in their original keys. 410pp. 9 x 12. 0-486-23482-7

THE AWAKENING, Kate Chopin. First published in 1899, this controversial novel of a New Orleans wife's search for love outside a stifling marriage shocked readers. Today, it remains a first-rate narrative with superb characterization. New introductory Note. 128pp. 5³⁄₁₆ x 8¼. 0-486-27786-0

BASIC DRAWING, Louis Priscilla. Beginning with perspective, this commonsense manual progresses to the figure in movement, light and shade, anatomy, drapery, composition, trees and landscape, and outdoor sketching. Black-and-white illustrations throughout. 128pp. 8⅜ x 11. 0-486-45815-6

Browse over 9,000 books at www.doverpublications.com

THE BATTLES THAT CHANGED HISTORY, Fletcher Pratt. Historian profiles 16 crucial conflicts, ancient to modern, that changed the course of Western civilization. Gripping accounts of battles led by Alexander the Great, Joan of Arc, Ulysses S. Grant, other commanders. 27 maps. 352pp. 5⅜ x 8½. 0-486-41129-X

BEETHOVEN'S LETTERS, Ludwig van Beethoven. Edited by Dr. A. C. Kalischer. Features 457 letters to fellow musicians, friends, greats, patrons, and literary men. Reveals musical thoughts, quirks of personality, insights, and daily events. Includes 15 plates. 410pp. 5⅜ x 8½. 0-486-22769-3

BERNICE BOBS HER HAIR AND OTHER STORIES, F. Scott Fitzgerald. This brilliant anthology includes 6 of Fitzgerald's most popular stories: "The Diamond as Big as the Ritz," the title tale, "The Offshore Pirate," "The Ice Palace," "The Jelly Bean," and "May Day." 176pp. 5⅜ x 8½. 0-486-47049-0

BESLER'S BOOK OF FLOWERS AND PLANTS: 73 Full-Color Plates from Hortus Eystettensis, 1613, Basilius Besler. Here is a selection of magnificent plates from the *Hortus Eystettensis*, which vividly illustrated and identified the plants, flowers, and trees that thrived in the legendary German garden at Eichstätt. 80pp. 8⅜ x 11. 0-486-46005-3

THE BOOK OF KELLS, Edited by Blanche Cirker. Painstakingly reproduced from a rare facsimile edition, this volume contains full-page decorations, portraits, illustrations, plus a sampling of textual leaves with exquisite calligraphy and ornamentation. 32 full-color illustrations. 32pp. 9⅜ x 12¼. 0-486-24345-1

THE BOOK OF THE CROSSBOW: With an Additional Section on Catapults and Other Siege Engines, Ralph Payne-Gallwey. Fascinating study traces history and use of crossbow as military and sporting weapon, from Middle Ages to modern times. Also covers related weapons: balistas, catapults, Turkish bows, more. Over 240 illustrations. 400pp. 7¼ x 10⅛. 0-486-28720-3

THE BUNGALOW BOOK: Floor Plans and Photos of 112 Houses, 1910, Henry L. Wilson. Here are 112 of the most popular and economic blueprints of the early 20th century — plus an illustration or photograph of each completed house. A wonderful time capsule that still offers a wealth of valuable insights. 160pp. 8⅜ x 11. 0-486-45104-6

THE CALL OF THE WILD, Jack London. A classic novel of adventure, drawn from London's own experiences as a Klondike adventurer, relating the story of a heroic dog caught in the brutal life of the Alaska Gold Rush. Note. 64pp. 5³⁄₁₆ x 8¼. 0-486-26472-6

CANDIDE, Voltaire. Edited by Francois-Marie Arouet. One of the world's great satires since its first publication in 1759. Witty, caustic skewering of romance, science, philosophy, religion, government — nearly all human ideals and institutions. 112pp. 5³⁄₁₆ x 8¼. 0-486-26689-3

CELEBRATED IN THEIR TIME: Photographic Portraits from the George Grantham Bain Collection, Edited by Amy Pastan. With an Introduction by Michael Carlebach. Remarkable portrait gallery features 112 rare images of Albert Einstein, Charlie Chaplin, the Wright Brothers, Henry Ford, and other luminaries from the worlds of politics, art, entertainment, and industry. 128pp. 8⅜ x 11. 0-486-46754-6

CHARIOTS FOR APOLLO: The NASA History of Manned Lunar Spacecraft to 1969, Courtney G. Brooks, James M. Grimwood, and Loyd S. Swenson, Jr. This illustrated history by a trio of experts is the definitive reference on the Apollo spacecraft and lunar modules. It traces the vehicles' design, development, and operation in space. More than 100 photographs and illustrations. 576pp. 6¾ x 9¼. 0-486-46756-2

Browse over 9,000 books at www.doverpublications.com

A CHRISTMAS CAROL, Charles Dickens. This engrossing tale relates Ebenezer Scrooge's ghostly journeys through Christmases past, present, and future and his ultimate transformation from a harsh and grasping old miser to a charitable and compassionate human being. 80pp. 5³⁄₁₆ x 8¼.   0-486-26865-9

COMMON SENSE, Thomas Paine. First published in January of 1776, this highly influential landmark document clearly and persuasively argued for American separation from Great Britain and paved the way for the Declaration of Independence. 64pp. 5³⁄₁₆ x 8¼.   0-486-29602-4

THE COMPLETE SHORT STORIES OF OSCAR WILDE, Oscar Wilde. Complete texts of "The Happy Prince and Other Tales," "A House of Pomegranates," "Lord Arthur Savile's Crime and Other Stories," "Poems in Prose," and "The Portrait of Mr. W. H." 208pp. 5³⁄₁₆ x 8¼.   0-486-45216-6

COMPLETE SONNETS, William Shakespeare. Over 150 exquisite poems deal with love, friendship, the tyranny of time, beauty's evanescence, death, and other themes in language of remarkable power, precision, and beauty. Glossary of archaic terms. 80pp. 5³⁄₁₆ x 8¼.   0-486-26686-9

THE COUNT OF MONTE CRISTO: Abridged Edition, Alexandre Dumas. Falsely accused of treason, Edmond Dantès is imprisoned in the bleak Chateau d'If. After a hair-raising escape, he launches an elaborate plot to extract a bitter revenge against those who betrayed him. 448pp. 5³⁄₁₆ x 8¼.   0-486-45643-9

CRAFTSMAN BUNGALOWS: Designs from the Pacific Northwest, Yoho & Merritt. This reprint of a rare catalog, showcasing the charming simplicity and cozy style of Craftsman bungalows, is filled with photos of completed homes, plus floor plans and estimated costs. An indispensable resource for architects, historians, and illustrators. 112pp. 10 x 7.   0-486-46875-5

CRAFTSMAN BUNGALOWS: 59 Homes from "The Craftsman," Edited by Gustav Stickley. Best and most attractive designs from Arts and Crafts Movement publication — 1903–1916 — includes sketches, photographs of homes, floor plans, descriptive text. 128pp. 8¼ x 11.   0-486-25829-7

CRIME AND PUNISHMENT, Fyodor Dostoyevsky. Translated by Constance Garnett. Supreme masterpiece tells the story of Raskolnikov, a student tormented by his own thoughts after he murders an old woman. Overwhelmed by guilt and terror, he confesses and goes to prison. 480pp. 5³⁄₁₆ x 8¼.   0-486-41587-2

THE DECLARATION OF INDEPENDENCE AND OTHER GREAT DOCUMENTS OF AMERICAN HISTORY: 1775-1865, Edited by John Grafton. Thirteen compelling and influential documents: Henry's "Give Me Liberty or Give Me Death," Declaration of Independence, The Constitution, Washington's First Inaugural Address, The Monroe Doctrine, The Emancipation Proclamation, Gettysburg Address, more. 64pp. 5³⁄₁₆ x 8¼.   0-486-41124-9

THE DESERT AND THE SOWN: Travels in Palestine and Syria, Gertrude Bell. "The female Lawrence of Arabia," Gertrude Bell wrote captivating, perceptive accounts of her travels in the Middle East. This intriguing narrative, accompanied by 160 photos, traces her 1905 sojourn in Lebanon, Syria, and Palestine. 368pp. 5⅜ x 8½.   0-486-46876-3

A DOLL'S HOUSE, Henrik Ibsen. Ibsen's best-known play displays his genius for realistic prose drama. An expression of women's rights, the play climaxes when the central character, Nora, rejects a smothering marriage and life in "a doll's house." 80pp. 5³⁄₁₆ x 8¼.   0-486-27062-9

DOOMED SHIPS: Great Ocean Liner Disasters, William H. Miller, Jr. Nearly 200 photographs, many from private collections, highlight tales of some of the vessels whose pleasure cruises ended in catastrophe: the *Morro Castle, Normandie, Andrea Doria, Europa,* and many others. 128pp. 8⅜ x 11¾. 0-486-45366-9

THE DORÉ BIBLE ILLUSTRATIONS, Gustave Doré. Detailed plates from the Bible: the Creation scenes, Adam and Eve, horrifying visions of the Flood, the battle sequences with their monumental crowds, depictions of the life of Jesus, 241 plates in all. 241pp. 9 x 12. 0-486-23004-X

DRAWING DRAPERY FROM HEAD TO TOE, Cliff Young. Expert guidance on how to draw shirts, pants, skirts, gloves, hats, and coats on the human figure, including folds in relation to the body, pull and crush, action folds, creases, more. Over 200 drawings. 48pp. 8¼ x 11. 0-486-45591-2

DUBLINERS, James Joyce. A fine and accessible introduction to the work of one of the 20th century's most influential writers, this collection features 15 tales, including a masterpiece of the short-story genre, "The Dead." 160pp. 5³⁄₁₆ x 8¼.
0-486-26870-5

EASY-TO-MAKE POP-UPS, Joan Irvine. Illustrated by Barbara Reid. Dozens of wonderful ideas for three-dimensional paper fun — from holiday greeting cards with moving parts to a pop-up menagerie. Easy-to-follow, illustrated instructions for more than 30 projects. 299 black-and-white illustrations. 96pp. 8⅜ x 11.
0-486-44622-0

EASY-TO-MAKE STORYBOOK DOLLS: A "Novel" Approach to Cloth Dollmaking, Sherralyn St. Clair. Favorite fictional characters come alive in this unique beginner's dollmaking guide. Includes patterns for Pollyanna, Dorothy from *The Wonderful Wizard of Oz,* Mary of *The Secret Garden,* plus easy-to-follow instructions, 263 black-and-white illustrations, and an 8-page color insert. 112pp. 8¼ x 11. 0-486-47360-0

EINSTEIN'S ESSAYS IN SCIENCE, Albert Einstein. Speeches and essays in accessible, everyday language profile influential physicists such as Niels Bohr and Isaac Newton. They also explore areas of physics to which the author made major contributions. 128pp. 5 x 8. 0-486-47011-3

EL DORADO: Further Adventures of the Scarlet Pimpernel, Baroness Orczy. A popular sequel to *The Scarlet Pimpernel,* this suspenseful story recounts the Pimpernel's attempts to rescue the Dauphin from imprisonment during the French Revolution. An irresistible blend of intrigue, period detail, and vibrant characterizations. 352pp. 5³⁄₁₆ x 8¼. 0-486-44026-5

ELEGANT SMALL HOMES OF THE TWENTIES: 99 Designs from a Competition, Chicago Tribune. Nearly 100 designs for five- and six-room houses feature New England and Southern colonials, Normandy cottages, stately Italianate dwellings, and other fascinating snapshots of American domestic architecture of the 1920s. 112pp. 9 x 12. 0-486-46910-7

THE ELEMENTS OF STYLE: The Original Edition, William Strunk, Jr. This is the book that generations of writers have relied upon for timeless advice on grammar, diction, syntax, and other essentials. In concise terms, it identifies the principal requirements of proper style and common errors. 64pp. 5⅜ x 8½. 0-486-44798-7

THE ELUSIVE PIMPERNEL, Baroness Orczy. Robespierre's revolutionaries find their wicked schemes thwarted by the heroic Pimpernel — Sir Percival Blakeney. In this thrilling sequel, Chauvelin devises a plot to eliminate the Pimpernel and his wife. 272pp. 5³⁄₁₆ x 8¼. 0-486-45464-9

Browse over 9,000 books at www.doverpublications.com